FIRED TO
HIRED

FIRED TO HIRED

**BOUNCING BACK FROM JOB LOSS
TO GET TO WORK RIGHT NOW**

TORY JOHNSON

BERKLEY BOOKS, NEW YORK

THE BERKLEY PUBLISHING GROUP
Published by the Penguin Group
Penguin Group (USA) Inc.
375 Hudson Street, New York, New York 10014, USA
Penguin Group (Canada), 90 Eglinton Avenue East, Suite 700, Toronto, Ontario M4P 2Y3, Canada
(a division of Pearson Penguin Canada Inc.)
Penguin Books Ltd., 80 Strand, London WC2R 0RL, England
Penguin Group Ireland, 25 St. Stephen's Green, Dublin 2, Ireland (a division of Penguin Books Ltd.)
Penguin Group (Australia), 250 Camberwell Road, Camberwell, Victoria 3124, Australia
(a division of Pearson Australia Group Pty. Ltd.)
Penguin Books India Pvt. Ltd., 11 Community Centre, Panchsheel Park, New Delhi—110 017, India
Penguin Group (NZ), 67 Apollo Drive, Rosedale, North Shore, 0632, New Zealand
(a division of Pearson New Zealand Ltd.)
Penguin Books (South Africa) (Pty.) Ltd., 24 Sturdee Avenue, Rosebank, Johannesburg 2196,
South Africa

Penguin Books Ltd., Registered Offices: 80 Strand, London WC2R 0RL, England

While the author has made every effort to provide accurate telephone numbers and Internet addresses
at the time of publication, neither the publisher nor the author assumes any responsibility for errors,
or for changes that occur after publication. Further, publisher does not have any control over and does
not assume any responsibility for author or third-party websites or their content.

PRINTING HISTORY
Berkley trade paperback edition / August 2009

Library of Congress Cataloging-in-Publication Data

Johnson, Tory.
    Fired to hired : bouncing back from job loss to get to work right now / Tory Johnson.
        p. cm.
    Includes index.
    ISBN 978-0-425-23055-8
    1. Job hunting.   2. Job hunting—Psychological aspects.   3. Employment interviewing.
4. Self-presentation.   I. Title.
    HF5382.7.J637 2009
    650.14—dc22   2009012496

PRINTED IN THE UNITED STATES OF AMERICA

10 9 8 7 6 5 4 3 2 1

To Evelyn Goldstein for teaching me that anything worthwhile requires hard work

CONTENTS

PREFACE

There's a good chance that you've come to these pages because you're out of work. Maybe you lost your job because of downsizing. Maybe the boss had it in for you. Maybe you picked up this book because you sense layoffs are on the horizon in your shop.

The first thing you should know: You're not alone. As I write, national unemployment exceeds 8 percent, and in several states it has reached double digits, with no clear picture of when the cuts will be curbed. The number of Americans who have been unemployed long term, which the Bureau of Labor Statistics defines as 27 weeks or more, is at its highest level in more than a quarter century. And the ranks of those underemployed—forced to take a part-time position when they prefer full-time work—has swelled.

The second thing you should know: It's not going to get better anytime soon. Even though that's not what any of us want to hear, it doesn't mean that hiring has come to a complete halt. John Challenger, the CEO of Challenger, Gray & Christmas, a global outplacement consultancy firm that tracks the employment landscape, compares the current job market to a "huge game of musical chairs—with more and more players, and fewer and fewer chairs." We all have to work smarter and harder to find openings and secure positions, and I'm here to help you do just that.

Although there's some small comfort in knowing that you're not alone, don't take that as license to throw in the towel.

Because giving up is not an option, make the decision—right now—to sharpen your skills and your attitude. The game has changed considerably. Job searching today isn't what it was twenty or even two years ago. If you want to get hired, you must not only be a qualified candidate but you must also be an exceptional job seeker, which is where many people fail.

In the coming pages you'll read stories about people—including me—who've lost their jobs for a variety of reasons: businesses closing, supply outweighing demand, a regime change, you name it. You'll read stories about how some of these people—including me—thought they'd never get another job. And you'll read stories about people who've come out the other side—including me—stronger, focused, and more energized than ever before. Not because of some epiphany or magical mantra but because they did the work it takes to get hired now.

It won't be easy, but we can get it done together. We're going to look at your strengths, shore up your weaknesses, and create a concrete plan of action. It's time to take control of your job search.

If you have a job now, you're crazy if you're not at least thinking of a Plan B. This is for you too.

Dog-ear the pages, scribble notes, complete the exercises, and mark up the stuff that's most relevant to you.

Dive in.

INTRODUCTION

When I was a freshman in high school in Miami Beach, my mother said it was time to get serious about my interests. She wanted me to get involved in something I'd really stick with, something I wouldn't give up easily.

The pickings were slim. I had no interest in learning to play chess, so that club was out. I certainly wasn't cheerleader material. Campus chatter revealed that all the cute, smart boys joined the debate team. Sold. I signed up.

In no time, I discovered there was something about debate that I valued a whole lot more than any of those guys. I liked competing and winning.

My debate partner and I became the first girls in Florida history to win the National Forensic League's state championship in traditional debate. When we took the top prize, our school, our community, and even the local media made a big deal out of it.

I have an article about that championship win from the *Miami Herald* framed in my office, complete with a photo of me—with feathered hair and with trophies in hand. As an eleventh-grader in 1987, I was quoted saying, "If you talk quietly or weakly, the judges will think you don't know what you're talking about. You'll lose credibility." When asked specifically about gender as we took first place in the two most prestigious statewide competitions, I told the reporter, "A lot of people were saying stuff like, 'Oh, they're girls.' But after winning a second time, I think people will start thinking twice."

From that moment, I had a strong interest in women's issues. I appreciated the importance of girls having the opportunity to compete equally with the guys, and I was proud to set an example for other female students. I knew at some point that this passion along with a drive to succeed would serve me well. I had no idea of how or when, but the seed was planted.

Today it's hard to imagine that it's been 10 years since founding Women For Hire in 1999. I find myself talking about the same issue of gender equity now as an adult businesswoman as I did when I was a kid 23 years ago. Does that mean I've found my true calling, or is it kind of depressing that the gender conversation hasn't advanced enough? Probably a bit of both.

One of my greatest pleasures is traveling the country to meet women who are focused on launching and advancing their careers. Some of them are just starting out. Plenty are out of work, much to their frustration, because of downsizing and layoffs. Others are reentering the workplace after taking time off to raise kids or because of financial necessity. I also talk to lots of women who are trying to juggle childcare and eldercare, without jeopardizing financial security or personal sanity.

Ironically, the current economic downturn has cost many more men their jobs than women. That's because the industries hardest hit—manufacturing and construction, for example—are dominated by men. The industries that have weathered the storm—healthcare and education—employ women, whose positions have been largely protected from mass layoffs. This has put more pressure than ever on both genders. Even if a woman is able to hold on to her role as a $30,000-a-year teaching assistant, her husband may have lost the union position that paid $90,000, plus exceptional benefits. Now they struggle to pay a mortgage, put food on the table, avoid losing their car, and keep creditors at bay while Dad searches for a new opportunity.

Because of this, the phone calls and e-mails I receive now come from both men and women. In fact, in New York, where Women For Hire is based, rapidly rising unemployment led to pleas from both genders to open our spring 2009 career expo to men. We agreed to do it for the first time in our history, drawing more than 5,000 attendees.

Another first for me: After four career books for women, I'm writing this for everyone.

These are uncertain times in America. But fortunately there are some tried-and-true methods for landing a job right now. Not only do I try to give my best advice when meeting people who are out of work but I also listen carefully to their ideas and tactics. I hear what works and what doesn't, and I'm able to pass along that wisdom and experience to others. It's my hope that in reading this book you'll walk away with several nuggets of inspiration and information to help you reach your personal and professional best. Sometimes it's the tools and tactics we need. Other times it's just the motivation we lack to go after what we want.

I've yet to meet someone who loves being a job seeker. Because it's not a role we relish, it's awfully easy to slink and sulk. Not good. We're about to embark on a journey in which my goal is to take you from *Blah* to *Ah!*

Blah is the person who can't shake the negativity that's thrown in his or her path. And let's face it, you and I can both relate to that. I've been there, as I'm sure you have too, and it's not a pretty place. *Ah!* is the man or woman who wipes away the tears and is ready to stand tall and do what it takes to nab the prize. Sounds easier said than done, right? Trust me, it's possible. So ask yourself: Who do you want to be?

In the chapters that follow, you'll learn to think like an entrepreneur—your career is your business. And if it's on life support right now, we'll figure out how to revive it. You'll meet professionals who have made successful transitions from down-and-out to happy and hired. They share their fears, triumphs, and hard-won lessons. You'll learn to recognize the difference between mediocre and extraordinary, as I help you find your place to shine.

Hmm. Maybe I could have been a cheerleader after all.

FIRED to
HIRED

CHAPTER 1

"Hello, My Name Is Tory, and I Was Fired"

Attitude is everything, so stand tall and get your ducks in a row

In 1993, I was a 22-year-old hotshot. Or so I thought.

As a publicist for NBC News in New York—the youngest ever, I was told—I was making enough money to rent a nice apartment near Lincoln Center, enjoy manicures and pedicures on weekends, eat out and shop. Not bad for a good Jewish girl from Miami Beach who had always dreamed of making it in the Big Apple.

I was on a roll. I had been offered a job working as a (very) junior publicity assistant for Barbara Walters at ABC's *20/20* while I was still in college. I jumped at the chance. Then NBC recruited me, and soon I was on a first-name basis with some of the biggest stars in broadcasting. Tom Brokaw, Bryant Gumbel, Jane Pauley, Maria Shriver, Stone Phillips, and the late Tim Russert.

This was heady stuff. At some point, all of those bold names benefited from my publicity skills for television's top-rated news programs: *Meet the Press*, *Dateline*, and the fortieth anniversary celebration of *Today*. It was my responsibility to promote these superstars and their work. I called newspaper reporters in every big city across the country as well as the producers of TV shows from *Entertainment Tonight* to *Larry King Live* to sell them on what my stars were doing. And the answer was always yes.

"We'd love to promote Maria's new special." "Of course we'll showcase that investigative piece on *Dateline*." "Let's plug Sunday's *Meet the Press*." I was very good at generating great coverage.

But it wasn't all sunshine. NBC News got into serious trouble when it aired a controversial *Dateline* story that showed General Motors trucks exploding into fireballs in certain kinds of crashes. But instead of actually capturing one of those explosions on tape, the story producers rigged a truck to blow up to simulate what allegedly occurred in actual accidents. A bad move ethically and journalistically, as an independent panel would later conclude. And an outright disaster in terms of public relations.

Defending NBC and *Dateline* kept me busy for months. I was grilled by reporters from around the globe from the moment I walked in the door of my windowless office at 8:00 A.M. until I left—hours after *Nightly News* had aired. It was a crazy and exhilarating time, and I loved the challenge. This is what public relations is all about, training I couldn't get in a classroom. I was truly passionate about my job. I loved NBC and its history and even the fact that I worked in one of the country's most famous buildings, the landmark Rockefeller Center. Everything about the job—the people, the frenetic energy—I loved it all.

Like I said, I was a hotshot. I thought I was really good at publicity. A rising star at the network. I was kicking butt.

And unbeknownst to me, my butt was about to get kicked.

Paying Dues

When Megan Henderson, a top morning show anchor in Los Angeles, and before that Dallas, was a television intern, she remembers "begging for extra hours, bugging the reporters, asking a gazillion questions, and annoying everyone around me with my enthusiasm."

"I left that unpaid internship and six months later I was offered a full-time producing job with Fox because of it," she recalls.

But today, Megan says, many of the interns at her station "just sit and wait to be told what to do. I always tell them, 'It's up to you to make this worth your while. If you truly want to be in this business for the right reasons and are willing to work hard, you will make it. But you've got to put in the work and pay your dues.'"

Increasingly, she says, younger people think in terms of immediate gratification. "More so than ever, kids are getting what they want, when they want it, and without a lot of effort."

But that's not the reality in most work environments, as Megan points out. That's why it's important not to get ahead of yourself—to trust the journey and know that you are where you're supposed to be.

"Working your way up is part of the process. When I was just starting out in the business, I was so focused on getting that huge market job right away. I was disappointed in myself for not getting to my destination immediately. What I didn't realize was that I was paying my dues for a reason. Had I landed that big market job right out of college, there's no doubt in my mind that I would have lost it just as fast. I needed to start in a smaller market so I could make mistakes and learn from them."

Megan says that she came very close to landing a job in Los Angeles after only a couple of years in TV news. "I was devastated when it went to someone else, but I now know that I wasn't ready for it. It would have been a total disaster."

The fallout from the GM story cost a number of people their jobs, including the head of NBC News, Michael Gartner. Before returning to his home in Iowa, he thanked me for helping him manage the story, and graciously told me that I would succeed at whatever I did. He wished me well.

I thought I was safe at NBC, part of the family. I had done a good job handling the GM story. I even talked to the new executive producer of *Dateline* about switching jobs and becoming a booker on the show that I loved. He said he liked the idea and would run it by the new president of NBC News, Andy Lack, a well-respected veteran in the industry who was hired with much fanfare to restore confidence in the news division.

And that's when it happened.

I got a call from a human resources representative who told me to report to Lack's office. When I walked in, he was sitting in his big leather chair. He didn't get up to greet me.

Not a good sign.

He clasped his hands behind his head, leaned back in his big leather chair, and told me that anytime someone takes over a company or a division, he or she wants to put his or her own mark on things—new protocols, new processes, and a new team.

The light dawned. "Are you firing me?" I interrupted.

He replied, "You have thirty minutes to leave the building."

Just as I did for the network with the *Dateline* story, I went into spin mode—this time for myself. Thinking on my feet, I told him he was making a terrible mistake, and I listed the reasons. Talk to anyone internally or externally, I said, and you'll hear what a great asset I am, that I really know my stuff, and that I'm totally devoted to NBC.

He looked at his watch.

Changing gears, I asked him to give me a chance to prove myself. "Give me three things to accomplish in three weeks, three months—whatever time frame you want—to prove myself directly to you."

All I wanted, I said, was to stay at NBC News.

He listened, cold, devoid of emotion.

It was clear that I was not going to keep my job. As I stood up to walk out of his office—trying desperately not to burst into tears—his parting words of wisdom were, "Tory, it's a big world out there, and I suggest you go explore it."

I walked out in shock. My world as I had known it had come to an end. I thought my career was over. I didn't even get to pack up my office. It was done for me and my boxes were messengered to my apartment later that day.

I walked to my apartment, climbed into my pajamas and threw myself a good old-fashioned pity party, catered by Häagen-Dazs. The entertainment? Daytime TV, long conversations with my mom in Florida, and lots of sleepless nights filled with self-doubt.

I was embarrassed, humiliated, and just plain scared. Word travels quickly in the world of network news publicity. I felt as if I could hear the whispers of "Tory got fired" down the hallways of NBC. Except I didn't—no whispers, no gossip, no words of encouragement—because my phone didn't ring. I can count on the fingers of one hand how many of my so-called "friends" reached out to me. Ouch.

Not long after, I got a kind e-mail from a former colleague, who is one of the classiest women I've ever met: Maria Shriver, now California's first lady but back then a correspondent for NBC News, based in Los Angeles.

She told me that I probably wouldn't believe it now—nor would I want to hear it—but that in no time I'd look back and realize that this was one of the best things that ever happened to me.

I deleted the message—angrily. How could this successful, rich, powerful Kennedy girl, the gorgeous wife of a movie star, know how I felt? What did she know about having the carpet ripped out from under her, about being afraid where the next month's rent would come from?

But there's a reason Maria succeeds at whatever she does. She's no dummy. After the benefit of some distance—okay, a lot of distance—I realized she was absolutely right. This was indeed the best thing that could have happened to me.

Yet at that moment, I was still too hurt and bitter to grasp her well-meaning thought. And it was those same feelings that stopped me from picking up the phone and calling the friends and colleagues who could help me get back into the game.

Blah: "All my friends were work friends."

Ah!: "True friends stand by me in good times and bad. This is the perfect time to realize who they really are."

Instead, my pity party turned into a misery marathon for months, financed by my severance pay, unemployment benefits, and my cashed-out 401(k)—something only someone in her twenties would think was a great idea.

Wallow for a Day, Then Move On

Radio psychologist Joy Browne says she was fired twice in her life and that in both cases it was the best thing.

"It never feels that way at the time, and everybody can say to you 'doors open, doors close.' It's true—but it's not the least bit comforting," Joy told WomenForHire.com.

"When you get fired the immediate response is just to feel horrible by yourself for maybe about twenty-four hours; you know, wallow in it and then take a deep breath and figure out why," she says.

"If someone will tell you why you got fired if you don't know, that's very helpful," she says. "Talking to the person who fired you, certainly in an exit interview, the most important thing to do is to say, 'Could you tell me what I could do differently next time?' Sometimes there really are things we do that could be changed, and that's at least valuable to know. The more we know, the less likely we are to say, 'I'm a rotten person, no one will ever love me again, I will never work again.'"

With a cool $23,000 in my checking account, going to the ATM didn't feel so scary. That is, until rent payments, retail therapy, and more than a few cash withdrawals whittled away at those five figures. I could see that my out-of-work windfall wasn't going to last forever. But before I continue with my tale, let's talk for a minute about what may be happening to you.

About to Get a Pink Slip?

If you sense that layoffs are coming in your shop, you may not be able to avoid the ax, but you can prepare for the severance possibilities. If you're part of a mass layoff, your bargaining power is diminished because the employer will have a predetermined package for everyone based largely on length of service. If, however, you work for a small company or you're one of only a few being let go, you can—and should—have a say in what you leave with.

Severance typically includes cash compensation, which may come in a lump sum payout or the continuation of salary for a specified time frame, benefits, property, and outplacement services. Consider each one carefully before agreeing to anything.

CASH

There's no precise formula for determining a cash payout. Some employers will offer one to two weeks' pay for every year you worked at the company. Others will offer a firm amount, say, two weeks' pay total, for everyone. Commissions or bonuses that would be coming due may be included in your payout. Unused vacation time can be converted to cash if you're being terminated before you can make use of the time you earned.

A quick story: I heard from a woman who negotiated for an extra week of vacation after her second year at the company. When that anniversary came, she went to HR to get that bonus week on the books. The HR person told her that she had to wait another year, citing "company policy." Luckily, she had her e-mail automatically saved in her e-mail program's archive, including the message agreeing to that extra week after year two—sent to her by the same HR person, coincidentally. She decided not to make a fuss because she wasn't planning on using the time just then. Not long after this conversation, the woman was part of a department-wide layoff. When she discussed severance with her manager, she asked to have her extra week of vacation converted to cash. The manager said she needed proof of the promise, which was on her company computer. *The problem:* She was now locked out of that very computer. She lost the proof and the cash. *The lesson:* Print hard copies of every promise you receive—bonuses, vacation time, and promotions. Store the printouts at home for safe keeping.

BENEFITS

The biggest benefit is an extension of your medical coverage, paid by the company, especially because COBRA is very expensive. Push hard for an employer-paid extension so you're not stuck footing the hefty bill nor are you without coverage. If your employer has paid for other benefits—a gym membership, life insurance, tuition, or cell phone bills—those may be extended too if you negotiate.

PROPERTY

Do you use a company-provided BlackBerry, computer, or car? Severance agreements may include an extension of access to this property.

OUTPLACEMENT SERVICES

Many large companies offer outplacement services, especially as part of a large layoff. It includes expert assistance with preparing for your next job. Popular services include résumé writing, job search coaching, mock interviewing, and retraining.

Your employer may not offer any of this. It's up to you to ask for it. So when you get the bad news, don't sign anything. Instead, ask immediately for a copy of the severance package. Find out how much time you have to review the offer before responding. Treat that deadline seriously, but don't allow anyone to rush you.

You may have plenty of clout to ask for—and receive—more than what's offered. This includes additional cash, an extension of company-paid insurance, and use of property that's valuable to you. Among the points to consider when asking for extra:

- Did you leave a prestigious position to accept this one? Reference any personal or professional sacrifice you made to join the company.

- Have you been an exceptional employee? Strong performance may justify a few extra parting dollars.

- Will your help be needed beyond your last day? You can agree to help transition your work to a remaining staffer. Perhaps you offer to be on call for a month if questions arise that you're best qualified to answer in exchange for an extension of pay and benefits.

- Are you being asked to sign a waiver? In exchange for promising not to sue the company or talk publicly about your experiences, you can ask for extra money. If your manager doesn't want to read a blog or a book (think *The Devil Wears Prada*) about your experiences, he or she may readily agree to sweeten the severance in exchange for your silence.

Depending on the company and your role, ask about continuing in a freelance or consulting capacity to assist with a transition. This compensation should be in addition to—not in lieu of—your negotiated severance.

This is also the time to ask for a letter of recommendation from your boss. You can also ask the HR department to provide a letter confirming your dates of employment and indicating that you were part of a reduction in force, left the company in good standing, and are eligible for rehire.

The more they ask of you, the more you can demand of them. Keep track of your unused vacation or other accrued benefits because they may not, which means you'll have to bring it up. Stay up to date on media coverage of layoffs to find out the latest severance packages offered in your industry or your area. Talk to friends who've been through this and ask for a referral to a reputable labor lawyer if you believe you have a claim for more than what's being offered. Don't allow the emotion of the moment to paralyze your confidence in speaking up. The power is in your hands to get the most money before you turn in that ID badge.

Healthcare Expenses

For many people, the cost of COBRA to extend their health insurance coverage after a layoff is prohibitively expensive. If you're concerned about losing coverage, check with your state about less-expensive alternatives or visit ehealthinsurance.com. Some coverage is better than none at all. Nobody ever thinks he or she will get sick or have an accident, but when those unexpected events happen, uninsured people risk financial ruin. Safeguard yourself.

You may also be able to negotiate fees with doctors and pharmacies if you're no longer covered by a plan. At your doctor's office, before receiving treatment, ask about a discount for payment and a reduction in the standard fee because you're uninsured. When visiting your local pharmacy, explain that your coverage has changed and ask about special programs that provide significant savings.

Sock It Away

If you're like most Americans, you've always lived paycheck to paycheck, which can mean sudden shock when the money stops. There's no greater fear than not knowing how you'll keep a roof over your head, the lights on, and food in the fridge.

Even if you've never paid particular attention to money matters, now is not the time to turn a blind eye. Financial panic will negatively affect your job search and could lead you to make bad decisions.

Ask yourself these money questions. Turning the answers into action will ease an already stressful situation.

- *What am I owed?* File for unemployment immediately (accuracy and honesty are the keys to avoiding a delay or denial of benefits) and pay particular attention to eligibility requirements in your state for emergency extensions in case it runs out before you've found a new job. Calculate this along with the amount and duration of any severance pay, including continuation of benefits.

- *What do I have?* Make a list of the account balances for all of your assets. No matter how big or small, jot down the value of savings; checking and investment accounts; and 401(k), IRA, or other retirement accounts. Also make note of the amount of available credit on your credit cards and home equity account. Even though tapping into retirement funds is not recommended because of penalties, you should know what you have in case of a financial emergency.

- *What do I owe?* Now focus on the flip side. Make a list of your monthly expenses in order of priority. Divide the list into two columns: necessities and nonessentials. Rent or mortgage, utilities, food, health insurance, gas, and car and other loan payments are likely to be your must-haves, while clothing, premium cable, and entertainment are not.

Depending on severance or unemployment benefits, it's likely that while out of work, your monthly expenses may exceed your monthly income. What to do?

- *Cut costs.* Obviously dining out isn't an option when you're not bringing in the bacon. And the cuts should go deeper. Examine your bills to figure out where you can trim any excess. If you're paying for extra features on your phone or cable bill, downgrade now. Avoid canceling insurance at all costs, but consider downgrading the policy as an option if you're seriously short on funds.

- *Conserve cash.* Consider making minimum monthly payments on outstanding balances to hang on to as much cash as possible. Before making any new purchase, wait at least 24 hours before deciding if you really need it. Everything must go through the want versus need scrutiny. Steer clear of situations in which you know you'll be tempted to spend money that you can ill-afford at this time. When a pal suggests a get-together for an afternoon at the mall, counter with a couple hours of strolling in the park.

- *Contact creditors.* Ignoring the bills and avoiding contact with creditors is guaranteed to result in penalties. Instead, call to explain your temporary circumstances and negotiate payment options. This may include delayed billing, lowering monthly minimums, adjusting an interest rate, and even extending credit limits.

For one-on-one assistance with finances, contact the National Foundation for Credit Counseling, an association of nonprofit credit counselors (nfcc.org).

Hold the Excuses

Good Morning America anchor Robin Roberts says that she once came home after failing to get a job she wanted and complained to her parents that it was because she's black.

That didn't sit well with her parents—her dad was a Tuskegee airman, the first black military air corps, her mom was the first black person on the Mississippi State board of education.

"They were like, 'Sit down, missy girl! We love you, we think you're terrific, but you've got to realize you might not be good enough yet. Don't ever say it's because you're black or a woman. Don't look for excuses.'"

Robin says that this little chat has stuck with her over the years. "I never have looked to make excuses or find faults in others. I just try to be the best that I can be.

"As women, we have a lesser degree margin of error," says Robin. "I can't tell you how many times I've been places and they hired a black or a woman and for whatever reason that person didn't work out. And they're like, 'Oh well, we tried, so we're not going to do that for a while.' And I would say, 'How many white men did you hire and that didn't work out, but that didn't prevent you from hiring, you know, another white man?' "

Don't be consumed with wanting to be liked, Robin says. "As women we want someone to like us. Yeah, I do too. But you just have to have thick skin. Do not look for excuses."

Own Up to Reality

Back to my story. With my money dwindling and precious time wasting away, I had to quit assigning blame for my unemployment. I had to find a way to finally shake my unresolved anger—the intense, force-10 frustration I felt at being so rudely dismissed by my former family. I needed a vehicle to blow off steam, lots of it, once and for all.

The answer came to me out of the blue. I'd take a cue from the Dear John letters by out-of-love women, and I'd write a Dear Andy letter from an out-of-work woman. And I really let him have it.

Dear Andy:

You're a jerk.

As the new boss, you have every right to clean house and fire me. But the way you did it—with a dismissive smirk as you barely gave me five minutes to make my case—is forever seared into my memory.

I will never forget how you reclined in that leather chair, hands clasped behind your balding head, as I—a terrified 22--year-old publicist in my first real job—fought to stay at a company I considered heaven on earth.

"Tory, it's a big world out there, and I suggest you explore it," you said.

I have no other choice now, do I? But you had a choice in the way you treated me. Just because you have the clout to hire and fire doesn't mean you have to do it so coldly and cruelly. Your arrogance astounds me.

I can't help think of the scene in *Broadcast News,* where the creepy suit asks the guy he just fired if there's anything he can do for him.

"Well," says the man, "I certainly hope you die soon."

I don't wish that on you or anyone. But I do wish that what happened to me happens to you someday.

Mean people like you always get theirs in the end, but it often takes a while. I hope it happens to you real soon. And I wouldn't mind being there to see it.

Sincerely,
Tory

Not bad, eh? Wait till I tell you what happened when he got the note. You'll freak.

Actually, no you won't, because I never sent it. But that doesn't mean it didn't feel good—really good—getting that anger off my chest.

I still have the missive, tucked away in a safe place, not to hold on to my fury but as a reminder that it's okay to be angry when you're treated badly and to never, ever treat someone with such disrespect.

Writing a letter to the person who fired you—or who was responsible for your being fired—is an easy and effective way of making you feel better and stops you from spewing that antiboss venom to the very people who may help you get that new job.

Blah: "No job, no money, no hope."

Ah!: "New life, new energy, new way to focus on what I really want to do."

Lesson Learned

I learned a few valuable lessons from my abrupt exit—uh, termination. Here are some of them:

ALL JOBS ARE TEMPORARY

Even though we think of ourselves as permanent staffers, nobody holds on to the same role forever. All of our positions are somewhat temporary. At some point—whether by choice or circumstance—it is time to move on. Sometimes that happens sooner than we would have liked or we're stunned by the suddenness of the change, but in the grand scheme of things it shouldn't be unexpected.

LIFE ISN'T FAIR, AND NEITHER ARE COMPANIES

Sometimes you can do everything right and still lose your job. New bosses want to bring in their own teams or old bosses think that by letting some people go they'll shake up the office. The sooner you accept that simple workplace truth, the sooner you'll get over the shock of getting fired. Another truth even more important to remember: You may have lost your job, but you'll always retain your talent. And with that talent, you can get back on your feet.

MAKE THE MOST OF THIS SITUATION

But sometimes making the best of it is the only thing you can do. It's still hard to admit this—even to myself—but Lack actually did me a favor. Working for someone so disrespectful and dismissive of your talents can have an adverse effect on your life and career. Just as you should end a toxic personal relationship, you should get out of an unhealthy working relationship. If you are undervalued and unappreciated for what you bring to your workplace, it's time to move on.

Vice President Joe Biden tells a story about his father, who worked a variety of jobs to support his wife and four children.

At one point Joe Senior was employed by an auto dealer who liked to reward his employees with silver dollars. At a company Christmas party, the boss dumped a bucket of silver dollars on the dance floor and watched as his workers scurried to pick up the coins. Joe Senior left the party, his family in tow. He never returned to his job at the dealership.

His rationale: A job is not supposed to be degrading. It's supposed to be rewarding.

"That's how you come to believe, to the very core of your being, that work is more than a paycheck," Senator Biden said in his speech accepting the Democratic vice-presidential nomination last year. "It's dignity. It's respect."

Even if you still have a job, you may be one of the hundreds of thousands referred to as the *walking wounded*—you're still employed or you're underemployed, but the terms have changed. Reduced hours, pay cuts, and forced unpaid vacations or furloughs are putting the squeeze on your compensation. And while you're no doubt appreciative of that paycheck in these tough times, even as it shrinks, it's high time to kick your job search into full gear.

DON'T BAD-MOUTH YOUR FORMER BOSS

If you have nothing nice to say, don't say anything at all. Fight the impulse to tell everyone within earshot what a jerk your ex-boss is because, fair or not, trash talking your former employer reflects badly on you, not him or her. So vent your anger in a Dear Andy letter of your own. You'll find a place to write yours at the end of this chapter, along with a little help to get you started. When you need to talk about your hurt feelings or your fears for the future, confide in a trusted family member or friend. It may take a day, a week, a month or even a few months to get there, but once you make that cognitive shift and decide to permanently move on, I promise life will get better. It's the first step in restoring your confidence and ego—two things you will need when you seriously and effectively look for a new job.

Just Do Your Job

Whenever anyone asks *Good Morning America Radio* host Hilarie Barsky about work advice, something her dad told her early in her career comes to mind.

"He was a tough guy who was very respectful of hard work," she says, and he urged her to "avoid petty office politics, gossip, and other people's drama."

" 'Don't put your angst on others, don't let their angst rub off on you, and don't be bogged down by all of their stuff,' " says Hilarie, whose program airs on XM Satellite Radio.

Another bit of advice from her dad: "Go to work. Do a good job. Get your money. And get the #$@#$ out of there."

She took his words to heart. "I resist the urge to respond in the moment, and I'm not a confrontational person," she says. "I won't go tit for tat when someone else gets moody or frustrated. I'll bite my tongue."

Silence Can Be Golden

During her early years as a writer, Joanne Gordon felt she had to prove to others what she knew.

That was ironic, the former *Forbes* staffer says, "since there was so much I did not know."

As a result, Joanne says she probably "did more talking than listening in interviews, in meetings, and in performance reviews. I not only missed opportunities to grow, but I'm sure I failed to impress. I wish I knew that it is okay not to have answers, or to voice them if I did."

No one ever told her that she was talking too much, but one day she heard someone say that whenever she heard herself talking she stopped because it was a clue she'd gone on too long. "I adopted it for myself. When I did talk less nothing was lost, only gained. Less is more."

These days, Joanne says she embraces her ignorance. "Then I ask, listen, and learn. And the moment I hear myself talking too much, I try to shut up."

Get on Your Way

Now it's time to get to work. Here are some tips to start you off on your path toward securing a new job. Write these tips down and post them on the fridge or the bathroom mirror—any place where you will see them every day.

DO NOT PANIC

Getting anxious about what you perceive as a hopeless, dismal situation or your inability to find a job is counterproductive. Nip it. It only increases your stress level—the last thing you need right now.

Stay calm and in control of your emotions, because a levelheaded you is much more effective than a frantic, frazzled you.

SET THAT ALARM

Like to stay up late and sleep past noon? Great! That's what weekends are for. During the week, you have a new gig—it's called "Find a Job," and you have to get out of bed in the morning to do it. Now you're working for the most important client you'll ever have: you. Also, you don't want to miss a phone call from a prospective employer because you were asleep, nor do you want to answer that phone with a groggy voice because an HR person woke you up. This is not a vacation; this is the time to dedicate yourself to finding something better for you and your life.

PUNCH THE CLOCK

It's natural to goof off while job hunting but it's important to approach your job search like a professional. That means putting yourself on a regular schedule. Wake up early, shower, get dressed, and have breakfast, just as you would do if you were heading out to an office. Map out a period of time each day—I recommend a minimum of four hours—during which you do nothing but make networking calls and follow-ups, check online job boards, or meet professional connections. You'll be amazed at what you can accomplish in as little as four hours a day. By focusing on your job search as intently as you would a job, you're more likely to reach your goals.

GET OFF YOUR BUTT

Pounding the pavement is not the same thing as doing cardio. While plotting your new workday, pencil in some time for exercise, even if this isn't part of your old routine. Exercise will give you added energy, enable you to blow off steam, and help you avoid depression. An hour at the gym, a brisk walk in the park with your dog or a friend, or some downward dog in your living room will recharge your body and spirit.

KEEP A JOB JOURNAL

Buy a lined notebook to maintain a job journal dedicated to your search. On those pages, make note of at least three specific things you do each day toward finding a job. Keep track of the people you meet, paying particular attention to any required follow-up. Since successful job searching is broken down into regular and continuous baby steps that lead to the giant goal of getting hired, all of these entries will enable you to monitor your progress. Skipping days only delays your ability to cross the finish line.

End every day by reflecting on one thing that went right on the job-search front. Sometimes the victories may seem awfully small, and that's perfectly acceptable. You made a cold call and the voice at the other end was friendly. You sent an introductory email to a new contact and it wasn't returned "undeliverable." You added a new connection on your LinkedIn profile. Woo hoo! Don't belittle those moments. Instead, claim them with a smile. Every step counts and it's those teeny weeny triumphs that will result in the big payoff.

DON'T IGNORE THE PAIN

Loss of income can wreak havoc not only on your finances but also on your self-esteem. Men can be especially hard hit. If you were accustomed to being the main breadwinner, it can be emotionally crippling to admit to your family and friends that you're now out of work. Add to that the pain of not being able to take care of your loved ones financially. If these feelings are bottled up inside and they're causing friction among you and those closest to you, consider seeking professional help. If you still have access to your employee assistance program, you may be eligible for free confidential counseling. If not, contact your local Career One Stop Center or even a public or county hospital to ask for a free or low-cost referral. Until you take care of your mental health, it's difficult to put your best self forward in the job search.

Overcoming Worrying

For most of her career, Working Mother Media president Carol Evans believed that worrying about the problems at work was a necessary part of business life.

"I worried about everything," she says. "How would we reach budget? What if the CEO wouldn't fund my big idea? What would happen if my ad director quit? Is that new competitor going to ruin everything? What if no one shows up for our event?"

It was exhausting, Carol recalls, but necessary because if she didn't worry about everything, important things would fall through the cracks. "I convinced myself that not only was worry necessary, no, it was the secret key to my flourishing career."

Then about 10 years ago she met executive coach Mary Lynne Heldmann.

"I was telling her a few of my business problems and she was telling me how to handle them from a psychological perspective," Carol says. "The problems wouldn't really be solved by strategy and energy and proposals. They needed to be solved by finding a new and different strength inside myself."

Over the next year Carol worked with Mary Lynne on many issues. "It took a while for me to embrace the opposite of worry—

confidence—and to see that I could get much more accomplished with confidence than with worry."

Today, Carol credits Mary Lynne for helping her buy Working Mother Media and run it for seven years before selling it to the Bonnier Corp.

"It certainly wasn't worry that allowed me to do that," she says. "It was my strong sense of confidence—and sharing my executive coach with my management team."

BE PREPARED FOR REJECTION

I advised a job seeker to get contacts from the alumni association of his MBA program. The first phone call he made—after he introduced himself and mentioned the connection—was greeted with, "Just because we went to the same school doesn't mean I have time for you." This guy was so horrified that he dashed off a snippy letter to me for giving him the advice and refused to make any more cold calls. All this based on one bad call. You can't be afraid of cold calling; it can cost you many good opportunities. Be prepared for rude people to reject you, to let your calls go to voicemail, to hang up on you. It's all part of the process, and it can be very upsetting, but you can't let it get to you. Just pick up the phone.

Take Criticism in Stride

Years ago, before she became one of television's biggest news stars, ABC's Diane Sawyer walked into an TV station in her hometown of Louisville, Kentucky, and asked for an on-air job.

Answer: no.

"They said I wasn't polished enough to be on television news," she told WomenForHire.com. "It's funny, every time I run into the guy who said that to me he just rolls his eyes and says, 'Don't tell anybody!'"

Being told that you're not the right woman for the job—or that you're bad in your current job—is tough to hear, Diane says.

"The first few times it happens, you're just devastated," she says. "It just seems so mortally wounding."

In her early years, when she was unsure of her TV skills, rejection and criticism hurt.

"When I would be criticized for looking icy or of seeming like a snow princess, I would think, 'Well, it's not entirely wrong because I'm not myself on TV.' I didn't know how to be myself on TV. I was still too nervous and green, so that was wounding because it was true."

But as Diane became sure of herself, she learned to take criticism in stride. "You discover this funny thing happens, and as you go through life and it happens off and on, you feel it less."

For Diane, the litmus test rests in the validity of the critique. "If I don't think it's true, then it doesn't get through my radar. I don't even notice it."

ENGAGE IN A STRATEGIC ACTIVITY

Prospective employers and other professionals you meet will ask how you're spending your time. You'll want to have something smart to share with them. Two options: Enroll in a course that will support your skills development or introduce you to a new field. Another idea is to identify a worthy volunteer initiative and commit to long-term service. You should focus your time on a cause that's aligned with your career interests or in a capacity that relates to your career. For example, if you're in technology, volunteer for an organization that brings technology to underserved public schools or give your time to a homeless group that needs a technology pro to help with its internal back-office needs.

SET MINI GOALS

Job searching is a marathon, not a sprint. You won't nab the big prize overnight, so don't torture yourself trying. While it's important to be optimistic every day, you want to sprinkle that with a healthy dose of reality. If you wake up each morning obsessed about getting hired that day, you'll go to sleep each night feeling like a failure. But if you set mini goals—making five cold calls, following up on several résumés, and so on—you'll stand tall, pleased with your accomplishments.

REWARD YOURSELF

If there is a single self-help or motivational book out there that does not mention rewarding yourself for a job well done, then I have yet to find it. Looking for work is often long and hard, and there are elements of it that can be degrading as well. So it's important to set some goals and list rewards when you achieve them. Land a big interview? Treat yourself to a free career makeover at Sephora. You may even decide it's worth investing a few bucks to spruce up your look. Send out 10 résumés? Have dinner with a friend at your favorite "cheap eats" restaurant. Hit 10 cold calls? Order in *Nine to Five* from Netflix. You get the drill. Rewards need not be expensive, but the feeling you'll have when you reach one of your goals is priceless. And make sure to share your achievements with supportive family members and friends, who can help cheer you on.

REPEAT AFTER ME

I used to dismiss the power of positive thinking as some hokey gimmick. I was especially suspicious when my daughter, Emma, ended a yoga lesson and kept muttering, "I am strong, and I hold the power." But week after week, she'd stand taller and prouder—and even louder—when repeating the refrain at the direction of her instructor. Emma had a bounce in her step and felt good about herself. Months later as she'd struggle with a homework assignment, I'd overhear her saying, "I am strong, and I hold the power." Just those words—and saying them out loud—helped her get through a challenge. I watched Emma have her *Blah* to *Ah!* moment. Now it's your turn.

Time to download "Good Riddance" by Green Day or "Survivor" by Destiny's Child and start writing a Dear Andy letter of your own. In the box below, you'll find Mad Libs–style assistance. Trust me, you'll feel better before the song is over.

Dear _____ [*ex-boss' name*],

You are a _____ [*descriptive word you'd never say in front of your mother*].

I have worked for _____ [*the name of the company*] for _____ [*number of years*], often putting my job before my personal life.

I became used to your refusal to _____ [*a verb that shows appreciation*] my efforts and your lack of _____ [*respect, praise, or anything positive*] and complete disregard for _____ [*anything from your feelings to the good of the company*].

But I never thought you would fire me.

If you only knew what it was like to listen to your _____ [*again, something that mom would not approve of*], day after day, forced to follow your _____ [*something juicy about the boss' lame-brained ideas*] that were not only _____ [*nasty adjective*] but _____ [*even worse adjective*], you would be _____ [*how you felt when you first realized your boss was a jerk*]. I certainly was, at first.

But as the years passed, I realized that _____ [*something petty your boss prized*] and _____ [*something even pettier*] were more important to you than getting the job done well. Despite that, I continued to work hard to fulfill the company's promise.

Clearly, _____ [*anything from shared achievement to success*] is not on your agenda. Your expectations are _____ [*unreasonable? impossible? You get the idea*], your manner _____ [*time to make mom ashamed once again*].

I see my firing as evidence that you are a _____ [*failure, fool, flop—or another choice f-word*] as an employer, unable to _____ [*inspire? appreciate? recognize?*] people who are dedicated to their work.

In the words of the immortal Joni Mitchell, "You don't know what you've got till it's gone."

With no regrets and in all sincerity,

_____ [*your name!*]

What Comes Around . . .

Cosmetics queen Bobbi Brown is known around the world but there was a time when she couldn't even get a job at a cosmetics counter.

"I tried to get a job doing makeup at Marshall Fields in Chicago," Bobbi told WomenForHire.com. "I wanted to be a makeup artist at the counter, and they rejected me, which I let know when they come into my office wanting to carry my cosmetics. That's always a big joke."

It won't be easy, but I promise you'll find success faster with a positive attitude than with negativity guiding your days. You'll face numerous challenges in the weeks and months ahead, but you'll come out stronger and more resilient than ever, if you maintain that smile and stiff upper lip. Nobody likes a grumpy person, so you may have to force yourself since a positive, upbeat attitude is a must. Now let's get going!

CHAPTER 2

I Like Me. I Really, Really Like Me

Define your goal and hone your personal brand

After my post-NBC pity party wrapped, and I spent months searching for another job in PR, I landed a position as director of communications at Nickelodeon, the cable network for kids. All my friends said it would be a seamless transition for me because I was going from representing network news stars to representing animated television characters. "It's one and the same," they all joked, "it ought to be a breeze!"

I knew I couldn't rely on that cynicism to get me going, but I was eager to wow my new bosses.

So I jumped in and created a strategy to get media coverage for a new line of back-to-school gear that Nickelodeon was launching. Then I made calls to reporters with my pitch. Half weren't interested; the other half didn't return my calls.

I panicked. "I'm in over my head," I thought. It occurred to me that all my early success may have been due to the product I was selling—famous news personalities—was something everybody already wanted. Promoting animated characters on notebooks (this was pre–SpongeBob SquarePants) was going to be tougher. I couldn't help but think: "What if I can't do it? I sold myself as a can-do-anything hotshot. I've got to get out of here before they realize I'm a fraud."

I went home and told this to Peter, my husband. He listened patiently, smiled, and then reminded me that we relied heavily on two incomes to support our household. Unless I had another paycheck lined up, quitting was not an option.

Of course I didn't have another offer waiting, nor did I have any desire to get out there again. I was through pounding the pavement in search mode. Another *Blah* to *Ah!*

Blah: "I'm not cut out for this challenge."

Ah!: "I'm going to roll up my sleeves and give it my all."

So I sucked it up and started working. Hard. I threw myself into the company culture. I learned the protocols and issues affecting the industry. I invested in people, too, to make internal and external allies who'd help show me the way.

Ask Questions: Of the Right People

Anna Robertson, one of Diane Sawyer's top producers at *Good Morning America*, says that many young people like to give the impression that they know far more than they do.

"When you're young and trying to get ahead or pretending you're older than you are, you tend to act like you know everything," she says.

Anna says she wishes she had been more humble about her limitations when she was starting out.

"If I were to give my younger self some career advice, it would probably be to ask more questions—but only to people who can be trusted," Anna says. "I see many other young people who should be just a bit more honest about their understandable shortcomings."

Anna wasn't alive until President Nixon was almost out of office, and she was in high school and college during the Clinton years.

But in the network news business, questions about presidencies arise routinely, which can pose quite a challenge for an up-and-coming producer. What to do: Acknowledge your youth and inexperience or fake it?

"How am I supposed to know every detail of what it felt like during Watergate or what twists and turns happened when during the Clinton years?" Anna asks.

It took her a long time, she says, to ask older colleagues to share their memories, "which they always love to do," instead of pretending she knew things she didn't, or that she had her own war stories.

But Anna says you have to be careful about "who you de-humble yourself to" because in any workplace, some people pounce if they smell insecurity.

"You have to be careful to cast your questions not as an insecurity but as a desire for more refined awareness," Anna says. "After all, asking questions can be a sign of confidence and self-awareness."

While doing my homework for my new position, I stumbled on an uncomfortable truth about myself. I realized that I had become complacent and lazy at NBC. The job had become so easy for me, I could do it in my sleep. Now, faced with a new challenge, I was ready to turn tail and flee.

I had to work incredibly hard for every success I had at Nick. My time there turned out to be one of the best career experiences I have ever had. I had to hustle for every achievement, stretch for every success, and that knowledge made my accomplishments all the more sweet.

The lesson here: Success comes before work only in the dictionary.

The second lesson: When you earn success and recognition, you should spread the news.

All of which leads me to talking about the next steps in *your* job hunt (after you've taken stock of your emotions and finances): define your goal and brand yourself. A focused job seeker is much more memorable than one who can't articulate what he or she excels at and is looking for career-wise.

Blah: "What am I going to do now?"

Ah!: "I'm going to take what I've learned and find the job I've always dreamed of."

Define Your Goal

INTERVIEW YOURSELF

When you're going through a time of transition—code for "out of work and trying to figure out what's next"—it helps to jot your thoughts on paper about your work preferences. Take a moment to answer these questions. And then rank them 1 to 3 in order of likes and dislikes: 1 means you really enjoy performing this skill or applying this area of knowledge or expertise; 2 means you're lukewarm on it—you don't love it, but you don't dislike it either; 3 means you really dislike doing this type of work.

The difference between the following two questions is what you know and what you're good at. For example, you may have strong knowledge of event planning and one of your best skills is negotiating contracts with vendors for event space, catering, and entertainment.

What are my three best areas of knowledge or expertise?

A. _____ Rank _____

B. _____ Rank _____

C. _____ Rank _____

What are my three best skills—what am I really good at?

A. _____ Rank _____

B. _____ Rank _____

C. _____ Rank _____

If you've ranked your A and B responses with 1s, then there's a great chance you are clear about the knowledge and skills you can apply in your next position. If however the rankings are filled with 2s and 3s, it's probably time to think about what you enjoy—or what you think you may enjoy learning through research and training—versus what you know how to do.

CREATE A JOB WISH LIST

Maybe you know exactly the position you want to pursue. If so, that's marvelous. If you don't, unemployment offers the opportunity to think about your options and define a goal. Even though these are tough economic times, don't edit your dreams. You can pursue whatever you want and move in any direction you think makes the most sense for you. It's the perfect time to create your working wish list. Think back to the jobs you may have dreamed about. Recall the roles your friends have that you've often envied. Although you can write down everything that comes to mind, understand the realities of what's available in this climate. You can't embark on a successful job search unless you have a general idea of what you're looking for.

IS IT THE ENDS OR THE MEANS?

If you're thinking to yourself, "I'll take anything," banish that thought. That's no way to get started. When people use that line with me I say that "anything" could be a nurse, an engineer, a bank teller, or a professional clown. Would you like to perform the same job but for a different company in the same industry? Or could you apply your best skills to an entirely fresh field? Perhaps total reinvention is in order? (More on this later in this chapter.)

For example, a book editor could jump from one publisher to another. Or she could shift to a position editing a magazine or blog. She could also take her skills in a new direction, such as speech writing for a corporation or grant writing for a nonprofit. She may want to teach English at a community college.

I met a man who spent 30 years as a copywriter in advertising, working at just two agencies. This was the only industry he knew until last year when he was laid off. Unemployed for six months, he realized another full-time position in his field was highly unlikely. When we talked about the specific tasks he liked best, without hesitation he said he thrived on writing client pitches to land new business, which was just one of his many roles. That's just what a local nonprofit organization was in need of—someone to head its fund-raising communications efforts, which included grant writing and solicitations of donations from high–net worth individuals. Same skill set, totally different industry.

Ask yourself if you're willing to put your skills to use in another industry—would you be able to do marketing for a wine company after having worked in the marketing department of a children's software manufacturer? Quite possibly.

DO WHAT YOU LOVE

If you're unsure of what you want to do, think of people or positions that cause you to say, "Wow! I'd love to do that!"—and then talk to people who do it. Sometimes when you break down the job into the daily realities, you realize it's not such a stretch for you. Other times, you can scale it back to something tangible. Maybe you dream about being the next Roger Federer or Venus Williams, but you're not a star tennis player. How about working in sports marketing or for a Major League team or stadium? Your dream job could be found as a sports agent or event organizer. What about becoming a tennis coach or running a tennis clinic?

BE REALISTIC ABOUT YOUR INTERESTS

Maybe you can't be a ballerina, but that shouldn't stop you from pursuing a career in the arts. With a passion for ballet, perhaps you're well suited for a position in administration at a performing arts center. Sure, an administrative assistant can work just about anywhere, but passion for a particular industry counts for a lot. Don't settle for any old job; be sure you're seeking a position with the potential for leaving you fulfilled. You don't have to commit to it forever, but it should make you feel good for now.

BE REALISTIC ABOUT THE JOB MARKET

You may very well want a specific dream job, but it simply doesn't exist because of economic conditions. If you continue to go after the same thing without success, try shifting your focus. I've met people who've been laid off from six-figure jobs, unable to come close to replacing their income. Instead they opted to move in a completely different direction for the sake of getting busy and back to work. For example, think of the former advertising executive turned Starbucks barista because of a love of the coffee. Then there's the former project manager for a Fortune 50 turned Container Store sales associate because it's always been her favorite place to shop. When job searching you don't have to succumb to the self-induced pressure of finding the perfect thing. Because you're not likely to keep this role forever, this may be a good time to try something new with the intention of using the position as a stepping-stone to something greater. Baristas and sales associates get promoted, too.

WHAT YOU'RE GOOD AT VERSUS WHAT YOU ENJOY

If you're lucky, you're very good at what you love. But that's not always the case. Many times when you're job searching, someone encourages you to do what you're good at. Friends and family will tell you that you're so good at this or that, which is what you should pursue career-wise. And although being good at something is one way of looking at job options, it's not the only measure. For example, you may be great with numbers and accounting, but you're burned out from that line of work. Or you may be wonderful with children, but you're no longer excited by teaching. Instead of pursuing what you're good at, you now want to pursue what you enjoy. There's a key distinction—and it's a decision you have to make.

REINVENT YOURSELF

Because you have the blessing and the curse of being able to pursue whatever you want right now, it may be time to reinvent yourself. I say *curse* because it's often very difficult to decide what to pursue when you're staring at a blank sheet of paper. It's like when a friend says, "Where should we go for dinner?" You say, "We can go anywhere. I'm open to anything you want." It's harder to pick a place when nobody offers a suggestion.

Let's for the moment focus on the blessing. It's exciting to have the chance to rewrite your career path and move in a completely new direction. To help pave the way, answer these questions:

1. What three positions make the most sense for me in my head? (This is about realistic brainstorming.)

2. What three positions make my heart beat with excitement? (This is about "heartstorming." In your mind, the positions may make no sense at all, but this is what you dream about doing.)

3. When I look at this list of options, which stands out as the one I'd love to pursue if there were no obstacles in my way?

Now, using your response to question three, complete a "SWOT" analysis—Strengths, Weaknesses, Opportunities, Threats—to create a clear, realistic assessment of whether or not to pursue a particular path. This entails filling in a grid (see the blank grid on the following page) based on the following questions.

Strengths

- What's in your favor to support the pursuit of this position? For example, your best friend is in this line of work or you think about it 24/7 so you know you're ready for it.

- Which of your current hard skills can transfer to this new role?

- What soft skills (personality traits, leadership qualities, for example) would be relevant?

Weaknesses

- What skills and experience do you believe you're missing that would be essential for this role?

- What weaknesses would your friends and family point to when you announce that you're interested in this type of work?

- How long would it take for you to get the necessary training to break into this field or this position?

Opportunities

- What is the demand for this type of work in your area?

- Is this a growth industry or an area where there's a shortage of available talent? Find this information on the U.S. Bureau of Labor Statistics website (bls.gov) and search the position on major job boards.

- Who do you know in this industry who may consider helping you to make the move?

Threats

- What kind of competition would you face for entry in this line of work?

- What is the cost and availability of the necessary training?

- How would interviewers react if they saw your current résumé in relation to this type of work?

Do a SWOT analysis for a few different dream jobs. Completing this exercise won't offer all the answers, but it'll help you see a clearer picture of the road ahead. Do the strengths outweigh the weaknesses or vice versa? Do you feel confident in your ability to overcome the

SWOT Analysis Grid

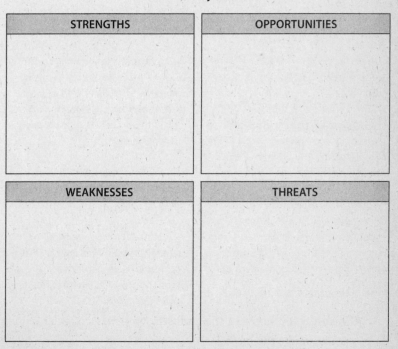

STRENGTHS	OPPORTUNITIES

WEAKNESSES	THREATS

My SWOT Analysis Grid

STRENGTHS	OPPORTUNITIES
• I think about my new business idea 24/7. I want to be my own boss and fulfill the vision of helping women to connect with top employers. • My PR skills will be a huge asset in generating coverage for my events. I'm also a good writer and solid communicator, which will be essential to convince employers to register for my events. • I have a thick skin about facing rejection. I know some people will say no, and that won't stop me from picking up the phone to call the next person.	• Unemployment is low and start-ups and dot-coms are stealing talent from top companies. Recruiting is highly competitive now. • More and more companies are talking about the importance of diversity recruitment and specifically outreach to diverse women. There's no other company producing career fairs for women now. • I have lots of media connections to help spread the word via print and TV, which will drive attendance to my events. I also have a friend who'll build a basic website for me.
WEAKNESSES	**THREATS**
• I don't have any HR or recruiting experience. I've never run a business. I've never done sales. • I don't have a deep cash reserve to cover me if things don't go as planned. My family relies on my income and I'm about to give it up in favor of something very risky. • I'm not yet an expert, so I see this as an ongoing learning process. I'll immerse myself in books, websites, seminars, and conversations connected to the areas where I must develop some expertise.	• The competition for recruiting dollars is fierce. I'm an unknown start-up going against well-established entities, such as giant job boards, college recruiting events, newspaper help-wanteds, and industry-specific events. • Information is readily available and easily accessible, but I worry about making time for research while working full-time. • Prospective clients may not respond well to "Women For Hire" and they may not want to take a chance on a first-time event. They'll wait and watch the first one before committing.

weaknesses and potential threats? The presence of obstacles is not permission to walk away from the challenge. While it's easy to get bogged down and discouraged when considering the weaknesses and threats, always ask yourself, "If not now, when?" Seek advice from friends, job club members, and other professionals on how to overcome them. If you really want to make it happen, the strengths and opportunities will outweigh the obstacles.

When I wanted to move from a career in public relations to start a company to produce career fairs, I completed a SWOT analysis (see my grid at left).

It revealed some very real weaknesses and threats, but it also showed that my skills, knowledge, and determination were even stronger. I wasn't going in blind. I knew I'd likely encounter challenges, but I was ready to tackle them head-on. Only you can make the decision of which way to go. Don't force an unnatural fit, but don't succumb to obstacles either.

Stepping-Stones

Every job can help you down the road, says Samantha Ettus, author of The Experts' Guide book series and host of web talk show Obsessed TV.

One of Samantha's first jobs was in ad sales at a computer magazine.

She had envisioned herself as a future magazine publisher, so that seemed like a good fit. But early on she realized that being a magazine publisher wasn't for her.

"I liked the creative side too much to be focused solely on the business side," she says.

But she stayed at that job for two years anyway, enduring the grind of weekly sales-training sessions and high-pressure quarterly sales goals.

Looking back, she says this gig helped make her books—which tap into experts for their advice—succeed.

"Whether booking guests for my show or enticing famous people to write chapters for my books, the skill I rely on most is selling," Samantha says. "If I hadn't spent time in the trenches of publishing, I might never have the guts to pick up the phone with confidence as I convince some of the most high-power people in the world to work with me. Every job can be a stepping-stone to a fruitful career."

Once you've pinpointed the area you're interested in or the type of job opportunity you want to pursue, it's time to skim through job postings. Doing this now will help you craft your résumé and your pitch. (We'll get specific about that coming up.) You won't start applying for jobs at this point. Rather, this is a chance for you to see what's out there—who is hiring and what those employers are looking for. Does the job you're looking for exist? Does your experience align with what's out there?

You can find this information by scanning the Sunday help-wanted ads, searching online job boards, and visiting the jobs section of the websites of employers in your area. Use social networking tools like LinkedIn, Twitter, and Facebook too. Since many jobs are never advertised, word-of-mouth networking is also important. Once you're up to speed on what some companies are looking for and what those jobs require of you, you can focus on the marketing campaign that will help you work toward getting the job you want.

Creating Your Personal Brand

Anytime a company readies the launch of a new product, it creates an array of marketing materials to support the debut. We are going to do the same thing, but instead of a new sneaker or a new movie, the product we're pushing is *you*. Here's how to do it.

CREATE AN "I ROCK" FILE

Can't remember your successes? It happens. We're all so busy that our workload often forces us to move on before enjoying our victories. Instead of passing off your successes with a simple, "I come through in the clutch," let's start compiling all those golden moments in an "I Rock" file today.

This is the place to store hard copies of e-mails or notes from colleagues or clients thanking you for a job well done. It doesn't have to be a formal note: a quick e-mail saying that you saved the day deserves to be printed. Or, to save some paper, store e-mail in an e-folder that you can create within your personal e-mail account. Anything that points to an accomplishment you're proud of—sales figures you generated, a tricky customer complaint that you handled, the rising grades of the students you teach, the publicity you score—should be noted and put in that file. You'll want it when you go in for your annual review, writing your résumé or revving yourself up for a job interview.

CREATING A SOLID PITCH

You'll thank your "I Rock" file when you are introduced to an executive at an industry event or a recruiter you meet when you're out to lunch with a friend. In those few moments, you have to be able to introduce who you are and what you offer.

Practice two versions of this pitch: the 10-second, handshake-long pitch and the 30-second, riding-up-in-the-elevator-long pitch.

What can you say in 10 seconds? More than you think. Here's what I say today over a handshake:

I run Women For Hire, which provides recruitment services for leading employers and professional women.

Here's my 30-second elevator version:

I run Women For Hire, which provides recruitment services for leading employers and professional women. I'm also the workplace contributor on *Good Morning America,* which is an exciting hat I get to wear because it enables me to cover a range of subjects that matter most to workers nationwide. I'm always interested in hearing from people about what works for their careers and why.

If my business suddenly went bust, here's how the revised versions would sound:

Short: For 10 years my passion as a small business owner has been assisting the best employers with their diversity recruitment strategies.

Longer: For 10 years my passion as a small business owner has been assisting the best employers with their diversity recruitment strategies. Through my role running Women For Hire and serving as the workplace contributor on *Good Morning America,* I worked directly with thousands of women—from college seniors to experienced professionals—to help them launch and advance their careers.

Let's say you were recently laid off. Don't shy away from saying so. Whenever possible, include the size of the layoff. If you were let go along with several other staffers, mention it. For example, "I've spent the last three years working in marketing at XYZ for the small enterprise division. While I loved my position and had a wonderful relationship with my manager, our entire department was eliminated as part of a thousand-plus-person layoff. We did some great work, and I look forward to leveraging all of that experience in my next position."

If you were one of just two people laid off from a five-person company, you can finesse it just the same. "I headed business development for a small paper products company. Because of the economic conditions, almost half of the positions were eliminated. But my time there enabled me to generate more than a $100,000 of new business and increase current clients by more than twenty percent. That will serve me well in my next position."

If you've been laid off for over a year, your initial explanation should not reference how long you've been out of work. Save that until you're asked. Instead, focus on the kind of work you do and what you're looking for.

No matter what your circumstance, you should be conversational, positive, and upbeat, which is all anyone wants to hear. Provide an instant snapshot of the general work you do, without pleading for a job in your opening line. Think conversation starter. Don't tell them everything, just enough to pique their interest so they'll ask to know more. Look through that "I Rock" file and create your 10- and 30-second pitches. Keep them in mind and always ready when you meet someone new so you're not tongue tied.

VOICE AND DEMEANOR

What you say isn't the only consideration. How you say it is often even more important. Leave yourself a voicemail message on your cell phone along these lines. "Hi, it's [your name] calling at the suggestion of Tory Johnson. My number is [your number]. I spent two years at a small production company, and Tory said you'd be a great person for me to talk to about digital media, and she also thought I'd have some good insights to offer you. I hope you're willing to give me a call when you have a moment. Thanks for your time and consideration. Bye."

Now play back the message. How would you rate the enthusiasm and positive vibe of the caller? Upbeat or a big downer? Would you return that call if it were left for you?

Record it as many times as necessary until you nail the proper tone. It helps to smile and even stand tall when leaving messages. Look in the mirror while you're talking and pretend you're being watched, not just heard.

Promoting Yourself and Your Brand

In the world of job searching and self-promotion, specificity is so scarce—and that's not a good thing. Instead of being generic, aim to be deliberate and focused when you're pitching yourself using any of your marketing materials.

CREATE A CARD

Business cards are a must. You don't want to find yourself writing your phone number on a matchbook when you meet an executive who may be hiring. Business cards are low cost but high impact; they help you present yourself professionally.

Cards must have all of your up-to-date contact information—name, address, numbers, and e-mail. No cross-outs. The type should be easy to read. Include something to help the recipient remember you such as your industry, profession, or even a photo. WomenForHire.com features special templates for resume business cards.

Use a card case to keep a supply of cards in mint condition at the ready.

DEVELOP YOUR DIGITAL IDENTITY

The Internet offers countless opportunities to get your name out there. Every job seeker (and all working professionals too) should create a LinkedIn profile. The site says nearly 20 million people from around the country, representing 150 industries, use the service. Not only do individuals connect with one another, but headhunters, employers, and business leaders search keywords on the site to find professionals with key expertise.

Another popular site is Facebook, which has more than 45 million U.S. users, enabling us to keep up with friends, meet new ones, and connect with leads in various fields. The "network" option shows thousands of companies, universities, common interests, and cities—categories that can help you find new contacts in your industry and reestablish ties with former co-workers. Search for me and send me a "friend" request. You can also join the Women For Hire groups on LinkedIn and Facebook to network.

Blah: Missing a golden opportunity to reconnect. Here's a message I received via Facebook from a former co-worker, whom I hadn't seen in more than 11 years:

SUBJECT: I need help!

Hi Tory. How are you? I would love to get together with you soon and catch up! Actually, I'd like to get your advice on a few things if it's OK, and fill you in on what I'm doing. I'm done with maternity leave in a week and a half. It's gone so fast, and now I need work advice quickly. Let me know if you have some time for lunch.

Ah!: Here's what she should have sent:

> SUBJECT: A blast from the past needs advice
>
> Hello Tory. I hope this note finds you well. Congratulations on your success with Women For Hire. I'm so impressed with your work.
>
> I am happy to say that I recently had a baby and now am ready to rejoin the workforce. I have found a great deal of good advice on your website, which I plan to put into action. I wonder if you could find the time to let me take you for coffee or squeeze in an office meeting so that I can get the benefit of more of your advice on my situation.
>
> Thank you in advance for whatever time you can spare.

See the difference?

If you're concerned about how to approach someone with whom you've lost touch, LinkedIn makes it simple. Make the day of your contacts by posting a recommendation of their work on their LinkedIn profile. This is a great excuse to reconnect with former colleagues, clients, vendors or peers.

LinkedIn and Facebook are the first places I go when I want to make contact with employees at a particular company or when I go to a new city for a career expo and want to find the right people to help make it a success. It's crucial to establish free profiles that include your current credentials and highlights of your latest accomplishments.

An example of how important this is: I knew a woman who ran her own events marketing firm for 17 years. She got a divorce and decided that she wanted the security of a full-time staff position rather than running her own business. She went to meetings with headhunters and told them about her vast experience and expertise. Several told her that they were surprised when they googled her that nothing came up. She said she never really needed a website because all of her business came through referrals.

And while that made perfect sense, it's not the way the world works now. It's natural that someone will want to google you and expect to find something—especially for someone who is advanced in her field.

When decision makers look up prospective candidates online, there is a natural inclination to be drawn to someone they can learn something about. When nothing comes up, it can lead an interviewer to question your experience, think you're out of touch because you're not using the latest technology, and overlook you completely.

Twitter

Twitter is a free micro-blogging site where millions of users post short entries—a maximum of 140 characters—that are instantly available to others. You can establish a free account and search for friends, contacts, and even recruiters you'd like to follow. You can also search by common interests, hobbies, humor, and industries to keep tabs on the latest news. You'll find that people track you based on the quality and content of your entries. To get a better idea of how it all works, go to my Twitter page—Twitter.com/ ToryJohnson. I answer questions, share job-searching articles, post leads of job openings, and often solicit feedback on segment ideas.

GET STARTED ON TWITTER

1. Use your real name just as I use mine. Some people create monikers or pet names for themselves, but if you're trying to get noticed, do so under your own name.

2. Create a one-line bio that explains your expertise. This encourages other like-minded people to connect with you.

Within the bio, include a link to your personal website or to your full profile on LinkedIn.

3. Set your profile and updates to public, not private. Twitter is about sharing your knowledge and opinions with anyone who'd like to follow you. Keeping the settings on private negates that purpose.

4. Create interesting content. You'll develop an instant following if you post thoughts or links that are smart, witty, or valuable to the people you're looking to court.

5. Update your feed often. Twitter profiles can be updated from your cell phone, BlackBerry or any computer. It takes seconds to add a posting. The more you post, the greater the chance of building a following. You should also "retweet" the posts of other people when you find them interesting.

6. Use Search.Twitter.com to find potential job leads. Search by the keywords that someone in your line of work might use to advertise an opening. For example, a recruiter looking for a sales representative might use "looking for" or "seeking" or "opportunity for" followed by "sales rep" or "account exec."

7. Ask for help from those who follow you. Instead of saying, "I need a job," seek informational conversations. When you cultivate a cyber friendship, it's easy to exchange information and give and get help.

By using popular resources like LinkedIn, Facebook, and Twitter, you have the ability to establish and maintain a digital identity and an online profile that you can control. You can choose the type of professional information that is made available about you. It can be as simple as creating a profile that mirrors your résumé and includes your latest accomplishments and experiences (good thing you have that "I Rock" file!).

Don't be scared off by the technology. If you set up an e-mail account, you will be able to follow the simple instructions to create a LinkedIn and Facebook profile. They're both free and each offers easy-to-follow tutorials on best practices to maximize the professional benefits.

Within your profiles—Twitter, LinkedIn, and Facebook—post a picture of yourself. Stick to something professional, not scantily clad shots from your vacation at the beach. You want to create a recognizable identity that may be viewed by professionals connected to your field or by those you meet at an industry function, career fair, or job interview. At the very least, set your privacy settings so you control who can see what within your profile.

The contents of every profile must be employer-ready. By that I mean, all of the content must be suitable for your next boss to see and read. Before I meet a prospective candidate, I check to see if he or she has online profiles. Sometimes I'm impressed. Other times I've passed on an applicant because the content raises questions about his or her judgment. Whether that's fair or unfair, it's a reality.

Think about Olympic champion Michael Phelps. He made embarrassing headlines when a photo surfaced of him, a gold medal–winner, smoking pot from a bong. Supporters claimed he was at a private party and his privacy was violated. Critics said he broke the law and behaved irresponsibly. The mistake damaged his reputation and brought about sanctions from the U.S. swim team.

In this age of digital dominance, anything about you can—and may—wind up on the Internet for prospective employers to see. Set up Google alerts (google.com/alerts) to have any reference of your name on the Internet e-mailed to you in real time. This is also a smart way to keep tabs on employers you're pursuing. You can set up free alerts on any topic(s) or name(s) you wish.

You.Com

Another way to create a digital identity is to start your own website or blog. Most e-mail providers offer website space and instructions on how to create a basic site. You don't need any special graphics or in-depth training to get up and running.

On your new site, you can post your résumé (minus your home address and phone number, share your views on industry events, reveal what you've learned at a symposium, link to headlines in your field, and invite others to post their thoughts. Keep it light, informative, and readable. If an employer does a Google search, he or she will see that you're informed, connected, and committed. Send the link to all of your appropriate contacts and ask them to bookmark it, contribute to the dialogue, and pass it on if they enjoy it.

Blog It

You never know where a blog might take you. Matt Drudge turned himself from a guy working in the gift shop at CBS studios to one of the premiere bloggers in the world of news and entertainment. The Drudge Report (drudgereport.com) started as an e-mail to friends, chockfull of gossip he says he overheard in the store. The e-mail was often ridiculed but always read. Eventually, the e-mail became a web sensation, often breaking stories that become headline news. What started as a snarky e-mail to friends has become a media-must read. Why was it so successful? Because Drudge turned eavesdropping into action—cultivating contacts, digging up information, and getting it out there.

You, too, can make a name and a reputation for yourself by

contributing to the conversation. Start commenting on existing blogs and speak at forums in your field. This is a good way to get your feet wet. Start a discussion group on Yahoo! or Meetup with others who work in your industry. Do what you can online to get yourself considered an authority about developments in your field. Begin your own blog, too. I like Blogger.com and WordPress.com to get you going.

A word of caution: make sure that what you post is something you'd want a prospective employer to see. Pictures and descriptions of your weekend escapades will not necessarily endear you to HR, unless they relate to your field. And trust me—every boss or HR executive will Google you and search both LinkedIn and Facebook for the scoop on you. So keep it clean and professional. A little restraint is worth the enormous upside to being so easily accessed on the web.

TALK—A LOT

In addition to talking electronically, speak before a live audience. Seek invitations to contribute your expertise on panels, at industry events, or seminars within your field. There are even opportunities for stay-at-home moms and new college grads to reflect on their experiences—it's not just for senior execs. This kind of experience not only gets your name out there but provides the long-term benefit of improving your public speaking skills. I don't know about you, but I've never heard of anyone accused of being too good of a public speaker.

Still not convinced you can do it?

Ask your kids or a college-aged family friend to show you the basics of social media. In a matter of minutes, you'll be up and running with the latest technology and your profiles will shine.

Looking Great on Paper

I trust at this point you realize the value of branding yourself in person and online. Now consider how you look on paper. Your résumé is usually your introduction to a prospective employer, so we're going to dive in to how to make you shine on the page.

I created a series of Great American Job Fairs as part of my role on *Good Morning America,* which have been successful in connecting applicants and employers as well as offering invaluable career coaching and résumé critiquing.

As we prepared to bring the job fair to Florida—one state particularly hard hit by the recession, with record job losses—I received an e-mail from Julie Brock, a successful single mother of three. She had been out of work for three months and feared that she wouldn't have enough money to make it much longer. Her 11--year-old daughter even offered to give Julie her birthday money, so that the family could get by.

Julie wrote that she had sent out countless résumés and hadn't received a single response. When I looked at her résumé, I could see why. Frankly, it was a mess—and she agreed it could use tweaking.

There was no summary paragraph at the top of the document, making it difficult to know what she offered or what she was looking for. In the experience section, there was no indication of her successes. It said she was in sales, but there was no quantifiable information of her performance, such as sales figures or size of her territory. Finally, it was poorly formatted and tough to read.

I helped Julie revamp her résumé in 15 minutes to reflect her tremendous success. She reposted it online and got three responses the next day, and a job offer shortly after that—proof that you can turn things around with a well-crafted document.

Let's start on polishing your résumé, beginning at the top.

REVAMPING YOUR RÉSUMÉ

Your résumé, a one-page (yes, one-page) document, is the first indication that you have the skills to do the job. It must be sharp, concise, and easy to read. A sloppy, poorly written document will end up in the circular file. Don't obsess on fancy paper, graphics, and other bells and whistles. None of that makes up for the content of the document. Plain résumé paper is just fine.

Contact Information

Contact information belongs at the very top of your document, so it is easy for the employer to find as he or she flips through the stack on the desk. You must have an e-mail address that you check frequently, at least twice daily. If your current e-mail address is along the lines of "hotfemale@hotmail.com," you'll need to create a new one for work-related e-mail that is professional. Create a Gmail account, which is not only free but also appears professional. Stick as close to your name as possible. Similarly, make sure the answering messages on your voicemail at home and on your cell phone sound professional. No music, no jokes, no adorable toddler chirping, "Mama's not home."

Summary Statement or Objective

Always include a summary statement. It acts as the "hello" of your résumé and offers the reader a snapshot of your career. "I want to change the world" or even "seeking a position with a multifaceted company that will put my talents to good use while enhancing my skills" won't cut it. This valuable space should be used to convey your core abilities and how you can apply them to an employer's needs. Make it as focused as possible in two to four sentences.

"A position in accounting"—okay, but boring. C.

"A position in accounting focusing on internal audit at Movies R Us, Inc."—too much. Save your interest in the specific company for your cover letter. D.

"A position in accounting focusing on internal audit in the entertainment industry"—short and to the point. B.

"CPA with six years of public accounting experience at Fortune 10 company seeks accounting position focusing on internal audit in the entertainment industry"—succinct combination of your background and the role you seek. A

An alternative to specifying an objective is to provide a summary of your professional accomplishments. This is particularly effective if you have a depth of knowledge in one or two areas within an industry. It's also a good strategy to use when you're networking and don't want to limit yourself too narrowly with an extremely focused objective statement.

For example, "CPA with six years of public accounting experience at Fortune 10 organization. Expertise in identifying opportunities for profitability improvement. Exceptional knowledge of budgeting and finance operations, accounting regulations, and strategic planning." This offers an overview without zeroing in on the role or industry the candidate is interested in pursuing.

Adapt Your Résumé as You See Fit

Résumés should be adjusted to suit the opening. You may want to highlight your experience in payroll if that's what the employer is looking for, or your aptitude for budgeting if that's what they need. If you have a varied background, look for a common thread among the positions you've held. For example, if your background includes working at a summer camp, waiting tables, and temping in different offices, you probably have lots of customer service experience. That's a valuable strength to tout on your résumé.

Experience

Don't list every job you've ever had in the "experience" section. The paper route when you were 12 will not help you land a job in graphics design. Emphasize the most recent and relevant, dating back ten to fifteen years.

If you've had a dozen temp assignments, list the names of the companies you've worked for, along with the agency, assuming the agency has not insisted on confidentiality of its client names. Make it plainly clear that you were hired as a temp, otherwise the employer might think you can't hold a job. If you worked at each company for less than six weeks, don't list the individual names. In such a case, list only the name of the agency that assigned you.

If you've held the same position with increases in title and responsibility, be sure to break out those promotions. Even if the differences are subtle and your title has remained the same, highlight the progression of workload. Think of a project manager. He may perform the same overall duties for four and five years, yet during that time he likely sees an increase in the number of projects he oversees annually, and the size and prestige of his projects grow too—all of which his résumé should reflect.

Articulating Your Skills

When describing the work you've done, show how you are a go-getter and a dynamic addition to any company by using words that convey energy and action.

Here is a list of some of my favorite *action verbs* that work well on a résumé:

Action Verbs

accelerate	coach	double	handle
accomplish	collaborate	draft	head
achieve	compile	earn	increase
adapt	compose	edit	identify
address	compute	educate	illustrate
administer	conceptualize	eliminate	increase
advance	conceive	enable	influence
advise	conduct	encourage	implement
align	consolidate	engineer	improve
allocate	contain	enhance	increase
analyze	contract	enlist	indoctrinate
appraise	contribute	establish	influence
approve	control	evaluate	inform
arrange	coordinate	examine	initiate
assemble	correspond	execute	innovate
assign	counsel	expand	inspect
assist	create	expedite	install
attain	critique	explain	instigate
audit	cultivate	extract	institute
author	cut	facilitate	instruct
automate	decrease	familiarize	integrate
balance	delegate	fashion	interpret
budget	demonstrate	focus	interview
built	design	forecast	introduce
calculate	develop	formulate	invent
catalogue	devise	foster	jumpstart
chair	diagnose	found	launch
clarify	direct	gain	lead
classify	distinguish	generate	lecture
champion	diversify	grow	leverage

maintain	plan	reinforce	structure
manage	prepare	remodel	summarize
market	present	repair	supervise
master	prioritize	reorganize	support
mediate	process	represent	surpass
mentor	produce	research	survey
moderate	program	restore	tabulate
motivate	propose	restructure	tailor
navigate	promote	retrieve	target
negotiate	prove	revamp	teach
nurture	provide	revise	train
obtain	publicize	review	translate
operate	publish	save	travel
order	purchase	schedule	trim
organize	quadruple	screen	triple
orient	recommend	shape	update
originate	reconcile	simplify	upgrade
overhaul	record	solidify	utilize
oversee	recruit	solve	validate
partner	reduce	specify	win
participate	refer	stimulate	write
perform	refine	strategize	
persuade	regulate	streamline	
pinpoint	rehabilitate	strengthen	

Spin Your Success

Now it's time to refer to and show off your successes, using both information from your "I Rock" file and some of the strong action words in the list. Instead of "wrote press releases," pump it up to "pitched media outlets, generating 80 news articles per month." It conveys the work you did and how successful you were doing it. Quantify that success whenever possible—"Increased sales by 20 percent," "generated $1 million of new business," "improved test scores by 10 percent"—you get the idea.

Responsible-Free Résumé

I can't tell you how many times I see the phrase *responsible for* on résumés. It drives me crazy. All *responsible for* means is that you were charged with a certain task. It doesn't tell me if you did it or did it well. Résumés are about accomplishments not intentions, so instead of "responsible for finding new clients," give it some muscle and say, "Secured 20 new clients, generating $10,000 in business per quarter" or whatever action words apply. Something as simple as a dynamic verb to describe your work will give your résumé an extra boost.

Now, take a marker and put a line through the word *responsible* every time it appears on your résumé. Look at the list of action words and use them to replace all of those big, bad r-words.

Key Phrases

When describing your experience, use current industry buzzwords and phrases in addition to action verbs. There's no chance that every résumé submitted online will be read. Instead, recruiters search job boards and websites like LinkedIn using keywords and phrases to find possible matches. There are also sophisticated automated systems that review online résumés and determine their relevance to a job posting. Before applying for a specific position, study the keywords used in the posting and make sure your résumé includes some of the exact language.

For example, when applying for a marketing position, it's not enough for a résumé to reflect that you've "led sophisticated marketing campaigns that have generated strong results." That's not going to be picked up in a keyword search.

It's more likely that the posting uses phrases like "search engine optimization" or "targeted demographic" or "ROI" (return on investment). If so, your résumé should include the same.

Recruiters aren't searching for "team player" or "track record of success," so while those overused generic terms won't hurt, they won't push your résumé out of the pile and onto the boss' desk either.

LinkedIn's Top Résumé Clichés

Proven track record
Problem solver
Cutting edge
Results oriented
Fast paced

Key Phrases That Will Open Doors

Strategic planning
Profit & Loss (P&L) responsibility
Performance optimization
New business development
Budgeting & finance
Corporate administration
World-class organization
Crisis management
Organizational leadership
Profitability improvement
Multisite operations
Joint ventures & alliances
Consensus building & teaming
Decision making

Streamlining efficiency
Best practices & benchmarking
Return on investment (ROI)

Education

If you are currently in school or a recent graduate, this should go at the top of your résumé because it's your most recent experience. If you're not a recent graduate or currently in school, then education belongs near the bottom. List your most recent degrees first. Leave off the date of graduation if you're concerned about revealing your age. If you didn't get a degree, include your years of attendance. List honors, exceptional course work, majors, and minors—whatever will enable you to demonstrate your acquired knowledge. Eliminate references to high school if you are in college, have a degree, or are no longer attending.

Skills and Interests

In the "skills and interest" section, include activities and skills that demonstrate leadership roles, honors, or special talents and abilities. For example, include fluency in languages, specific computer programming, or technical skills (not "computer literate"— that's expected). List hobbies and personal interests only if they pertain to the job or if one or two additions would be exceptional points of conversation. For example, if you're into extreme rollerblading or if you've traveled to every continent in search of the spiciest cuisines, insert that as one line.

Affiliations

Professional industry and volunteer organizations belong under the "affiliations" heading. Employers like workers who are involved in their industry or community. But be choosy—a day or two here and there doesn't count as volunteer work. If you've donated your old clothing to a cause, that's nice, but it's not résumé-appropriate volunteer work. It's always impressive to list any offices or special roles you have held in these organizations. This is especially important if you have limited experience because it can prove your commitment to your desired field.

Keep It Short and Sweet

Ideally your résumé should be one page. It's a document that showcases and celebrates the very best of you, not every single thing about you.

A Second Set of Eyes

Be sure you seek another pair of eyes . . . and a third or fourth pair. Ask friends and professionals to review and critique your résumé, not just for typos but to get a read on its overall effect. Make sure your objective is clear and that your experience as described supports the position you're looking for. Ask them if you've left any of your attributes out, if there's anything unclear or confusing. Who knows? It may just spark a great contact in their mind.

WHAT SHOULDN'T BE ON YOUR RÉSUMÉ

"I'm a real people person." Express your skills in a precise, unique and measurable way. If you are, in fact, a people person, explain it quantitatively: excellent negotiation skills, strong leadership experience, mentor.

"References available on request." It is assumed you have good references, so use that precious space on your résumé for something better. If the employer wants to contact your references,

he or she will ask. And be careful who you designate as a reference. I've gotten reference calls about people I've fired. Never use someone as a reference until you've asked specifically, "Are you one hundred percent comfortable providing a reference for me? And if so, what will you say about me if called for a reference?" If there's any doubt—even a wee little bit, leave that person out.

"Single female, early forties." This is not a personal ad. Your age, marital status, family situation, religion, and sexual orientation do not belong on your résumé. One exception: If your name is not common and/or if it doesn't automatically convey your gender, feel free to include Ms. or Mr. in front of it as a courtesy to the reader.

Don't be cute. Eliminate any indication of cuteness. Your résumé is a professional document. Pictures, symbols, or graphics don't belong here. If you're an artist or designer, that's what your portfolio is for.

Never lie on your résumé. My mother never lied about her age because she believed that anyone interested enough to try to find out, could, and being caught in a lie was much more embarrassing than revealing she was in her fifties. Employers can verify everything on your résumé, from education to work experience. Didn't graduate from college? Have a gap in your work timeline? Deal with it honestly. Never, ever lie because it'll cost you the job.

The template on the following page shows a chronological résumé. Use it to create your new one, and remember—no *responsibles!*

Résumé Template

Job Seeker's First and Last Name
Street Address, City, State ZIP Code
Telephone Number, E-Mail Address

PROFESSIONAL SUMMARY AND OBJECTIVE

Your professional summary is your persuasive sales pitch that introduces you to potential employers and allows them to place you in context based on their hiring needs. Compose two to four sentences touting your key capabilities and unique experience, with an emphasis on results. This section focuses on a combination of hard and soft skills. Tie your qualifications to the type of position you're seeking.

EXPERIENCE

Most Recent Job Title   **(Month Year to Month Year)**
Employer   **City, State**

Brief overview of the position's duties, including an explanation of the organization if it's not well known.

- Outline your most impressive accomplishments using bullet points. Focus on the results of your actions, not just your responsibilities. Include industry buzzwords and tangible numbers to support your experience. The eye is drawn to figures, especially on a sales résumé.
- Focus on leadership roles and demonstrate how you've found solutions to challenges.
- Start every bullet with an impressive action word, and vary the words throughout your résumé. Avoid fancy fonts.

Previous Job Title   **(Month Year to Month Year)**
Employer   **City, State**

- Keep position summaries short and relevant. A potential employer is scanning your résumé to see if you merit an interview—clear and concise is ideal.
- Don't try to include your whole life story. Outline your most important and impressive accomplishments, not a complete menu of every task you've ever performed.

- As a general rule, the amount of information—both summaries and bullets—beneath each position should decrease as you move toward older assignments.

Earlier Job Title   **(Month Year to Month Year)**
Employer   **City, State**
- Earlier jobs require minimal information, though they are important for demonstrating career advancement.

EDUCATION
- MBA, University (Most recent degree goes on top.)
- BA, College, 2002 (Date is optional, but usually included, especially if it's recent. If you graduated college more than 20 years ago, leave the year off, especially if you're concerned about age discrimination.)
- GPA, honors received (Mention your GPA only if it's above 3.5. I'm always turned off when someone has listed a 2.8. It's like screaming, "Hire me! I'm average!" Honors include magna cum laude and dean's list.)
- Leadership roles and impressive recognition.

SKILLS/QUALIFICATIONS
- This optional section can be used to enhance your summary and experience while highlighting specific qualifications that are either required for a particular job or are unique about you.
- You can expand this section when posting your résumé online to increase the number of keywords.

MEMBERSHIPS/AFFILIATIONS
- Professional memberships and volunteer work show your commitment to your industry and community. Mention leadership positions and briefly note relevant achievements.
- This is especially valuable if you're a recent grad or a career changer to demonstrate that you're making an effort to establish yourself in a new field.

COVER LETTERS

Yes, a cover letter matters. If you're applying online, there's often a standard form that doesn't accept a cover letter. However, if you have an option, include one. When I specify that all candidates should include a cover letter when applying for positions at Women For Hire, I mean it. That means no cover letter, no consideration. Follow directions instead of taking short cuts.

I used this ABC checklist in my first book, *Women For Hire: The Ultimate Guide to Getting a Job,* and it still works today.

A is for Assets. A cover letter includes your best assets but remembers to include the reader and their needs. Sum up your strengths as they apply to that company, specific job, and how you will be an asset to both of them.

B is for Best. Why are you the best candidate for the job? This is where you tell the reader why you're perfectly suited to help the company achieve its goals. Your enthusiasm should shine through and your letter should be compelling.

C is for Competency. You'll be hired for your skills, so be sure to address your competency in terms of things you are great at and promote what you know how to do that would benefit the company.

The following template uses those ABCs. Take it and make it your own. (*One note:* If you're sending the letter by e-mail, you can skip the return address, the recipient's address, and the date and just get right to it. Don't send letters as attachments to e-mails; just paste your text in the body of your message.)

Cover Letter Template

Your First and Last Name
Mailing Address, City, State ZIP Code
Telephone Number(s)
E-mail Address

Current Date

Prospective Employer
Professional Title
Company Name
Mailing Address

Dear (Address your contact formally—Mr., Mrs., Ms., Professor, Dr.—unless you were instructed to use the first name):

Introduce yourself by explaining briefly why you are interested in this person, company, or position. Do not begin with "Hi. My name is _____." Make a closer connection by stating how you heard about the person, company, or position by referencing a referral, an article, or an industry event, for example.

For the body paragraph, briefly give your background. Make sure it applies to why you are interested in this person or company. State what you want from the recipient. For example, "I would like fifteen minutes of your time to discuss _____." Explain that you'd be very appreciative of his or her valuable time and advice. Include ammunition about your credentials to convince the reader that you're worth it.

The closing paragraph should offer a specific action for following up. For example, "I will call (or e-mail) your assistant to see if I can schedule an appointment with you." If you state a specific action, make sure you follow through with it. Thank the recipient for his or her time and attention.

Sincerely,
Your first and last name

Only Rookies Wing It

Joyce Bone is a wife, mom, and successful entrepreneur who co-founded EarthCare, an environmental company that grew from zero to $50 million in 18 months.

But first Joyce had to stand up in front of 50 accredited investors—all men—and ask them to pony up $13 million. She learned only at the last minute that she would be presenting all the financial information.

"I was terrified because I was going to have to wing it in front of these men," Joyce recalls. "I was playing scenarios in my head like, 'These seasoned professionals are going to take one look at me and know I'm a stay-at-home mom playing dress-up as a serious business-woman.' I just knew they would be able to see through my feeble attempts to look in command of the situation. I was freaking out inside."

But then it occurred to her how ridiculous it would look if the only female in the room passed out. "I would be playing right into age-old stereotypes. Yes, I was the youngest and least experienced, but it was my idea and my time to prove I was capable and worthy of success. Fainting was not an option."

After her presentation, several men praised her thoroughness—and she got her money. (She later completed a Toastmasters course, never again wanting to feel uncomfortable speaking publicly.)

The key to winning over those initial investors was in her prep work, she says. "Always be well prepared for any presentation: Winging it is for rookies."

It's now your job to spread the news of your portfolio of accomplishments to convince an employer to invite you in for an interview and to ultimately say, "You're hired."

Are You a Star?

As you write each bullet of your resume, ask "What am I selling to a prospective employer in this bullet? Your answer should focus on a skill, competency, or result.

The STAR (situation, task, action, result) method is a helpful process to guide you:

SITUATION: Project was over budget by $100,000.

TASK: Analyzed budget for potential solutions.

ACTION: Evaluated budgets of other successful projects to identify opportunities for savings and developed revised budget with reduced spending.

RESULT: Reversed overspending to come in on target.

The final bullet would appear on your resume like this: Analyzed project expenditures and revised budget to eliminate $100,000 of excessive spending.

Now that you have your goal in mind and marketing campaign assembled, it's time to set forth and spread the word. No one, from your neighbor to your next employer, can see into a crystal ball to discover your strengths and accomplishments. Mom may think you're the bee's knees, but she won't be by your side to sing your praises when you have that interview.

It's up to you to start targeting a few openings, send out a strong résumé, hand out your business cards, and spread the word about all you offer. Extreme modesty has no place in any job hunter's arsenal. I'm not telling you to hire a skywriter, but you must be able to talk about your accomplishments and be self-assured. If you don't believe in yourself and toot your own horn, you could be cheating yourself out of the positions, pay, promotions, and perks you deserve—all because you're bashful about singing your own praises.

I hope at this stage you've convinced yourself what you're really good at—that you know your area of expertise and are ready to share it with the world. Time to get to work on your "I Rock" file. Listen to country star Toby Keith's "I Wanna Talk about Me" or the Bonnie Raitt classic "Something to Talk About," and make a list of 10 things you've accomplished at work that make you proud.

1. _____

2. _____

3. _____

4. _____

5. _____

6. _____

7. _____

8. _____

9. _____

10. _____

Make a copy of this page and put it in your "I Rock" file. An extra copy on the refrigerator door isn't a bad idea either.

Check, Please

As you create killer marketing materials for yourself, check off each one from your to-do list:

___ Mastered 10-second intro

___ Nailed the 30-second spiel

___ Perfected a flawless résumé template (Notice I say "template" since you'll always tweak the document for the position you're applying to.)

___ Drafted a strong cover letter template

___ Produced memorable business cards

___ Created complete profiles on LinkedIn and Facebook

___ Enhanced my digital identity

CHAPTER 3

I Told Two Friends, and They Told Two Friends

Networking for fun and profit

Have you ever been at a work-related function, where you and your cube mate are standing in the corner, sipping cocktails and watching a colleague handshake his way through the crowd?

Maybe you've thought, "That guy doesn't have friends; he has favors waiting to happen. What a suck-up."

Or maybe your friend snickered, "He's given out more cards than a blackjack dealer in Vegas."

All of which could be true. What's also true is that this man, who is getting acquainted with people in the crowd, is going to get ahead because he knows how to network.

How did you meet your best friend? Your significant other? You knew someone who knew him or her. Or you met at the gym or at a bar or online. That, dear reader, is *networking*. So get over the misplaced negativity associated with the word and get on the ball.

It was a lesson I needed to learn, too. I used to attend industry functions all the time because I knew it was the thing I needed to do to get ahead and grow my business. After scores of functions with no new contacts, I wondered if I really needed to keep going to these events. I knew that there was something to get out of them—successful professionals swear by them. What was I doing wrong? I replayed the last few functions in my mind and, finally, the light dawned. Although I meant business when I went to the events, I acted like a wallflower at a grade-school dance. I would bring a friend with me, and we'd stand off to the side and watch the action, talking *about* everyone instead of talking *to* them.

I was missing the point of these gatherings and missing opportunities that were there for the taking because I was clinging to my friend—as if she were a warm security blanket.

So I vowed to start going it alone. And I set a goal for myself—I couldn't leave until I introduced myself to at least three people. Full disclosure: I must admit that at the first few events I attended after this self-imposed policy, all three people I approached were waiters.

Finally I admitted that I was only fooling myself. I had to further refine my mandate: the three introductions had to be among people who were attending the function as I was. I still talk to the wait staff and security personnel because, hey, you never know, but I always find three others, too.

Blah: "I'll sit on the sidelines, watching others go after what they want."

Ah!: "I'll join the game and take the steps needed to get ahead."

Sing Your Praises

When author Debra Condren was writing *Ambition Is Not a Dirty Word*, she sent out an e-mail to several databases asking women, "What advice do you have for other women, and what works for you when it comes to the art of taking credit at work?"

Then she sat back and waited for the women to give their best advice. None did.

By nature or nurture, Debra says, women have been taught to view taking credit as selfish and wrong.

When a man is congratulated on his work, he'll quickly accept the praise, whereas many women will say, "Oh, it was a team effort."

"A woman fears being a braggart," Debra says. "She doesn't want to seem arrogant."

Debra says that there are times when you have to stand up, set the record straight, and take credit for what you have done—or risk losing out to someone who doesn't deserve the credit.

"You've got to tread lightly, but stand up immediately," she advises, and be prepared for retribution or backlash. Credit hogs are ambitious by nature and can be nasty.

"It's happened to me, and it isn't fun," she says. "But letting my credit be stolen would have been way less fun—so it was worth it to stick up for myself."

As I grew more confident, I started talking to more people and making more connections. Sometimes nothing came of it. Other times something terrific happened—a new resource, a nugget of information, a new friend, a new client, a new idea that may have never occurred to me had I not put myself out there to talk with people in my field. That's not the only networking lesson I had to learn.

When my twins, Jake and Emma, were in preschool they made a cute little friend named Michael. Michael's mom happens to be Kelly Ripa. And as the kids started playing together, the moms became friends. Week after week, I found myself around the fireball that is Kelly—at the park, a school function or on the phone arranging a play date. I kept thinking, "This woman has fifteen minutes on national television every morning to chat with Regis about whatever she wants. You have to ask her to talk about Women For Hire. Surely she could slip in a mention." But I was sheepish about asking for help.

Every time we had plans to get together with the kids, I'd tell myself, "This time you're going to do it." Then I'd let another opportunity go by. This went on for months. It never felt like the right moment. Looking back, I realize that I was actually waiting for Kelly to somehow read my mind and know what I wanted.

One of the great things about women is that we're natural givers and nurturers. The flip side of this is that we're often reluctant to ask for something for ourselves, and that holds us back. But you can't make it alone. We all need a hand and help from others.

And so finally, after countless missed opportunities, I gathered my courage. "Kelly, I don't want you to feel like I'm abusing our friendship . . . but I need to ask you something, and I completely understand if you say no, but . . ."

Kelly stopped my sputtering. "Just spit it out!"

I told her about some upcoming initiatives at Women For Hire, gave her the whole spiel, and asked if she could mention it on *Live*. In an instant, she said "Of course!" The next morning, Kelly and Regis talked all about Women For Hire. Since that time, she has been an incredible cheerleader of all we do because she has a really strong interest in and passion for working women. I couldn't ask for a better friend.

Build Networks Before You Need Them

Billie Williamson, a partner and Americas inclusiveness officer at accounting giant Ernst & Young, has always known how important it is to nurture relationships with clients and support people who work for her.

If you have good relationships with people inside and outside your company, stay in touch because you never know when you'll need help, Billie says. Send them an interesting article now and then or find other ways to keep in contact.

"The lesson is that if you care for people and help people, it will come back to you many times over in the future. You need to build your networks before you need them."

I realized I was hesitant to ask for help because I was waiting for the perfect moment. I can't even articulate what the perfect moment looks like; you just know it when you feel it. The problem is that fantasy of perfection rarely meshes with reality. We wait and wait for the ideal time, and it simply never comes. I've missed many opportunities because of this imaginary barrier I allowed to stand in my way.

Finally I learned to ask for things when the moment is good enough. That's not about lowering my standards; it's about adjusting for everyday realities. Don't wait for your vision of perfection. Most times the moment is good enough to speak up for what you want.

When it comes to having the guts to ask for help, my asking Kelly Ripa for a plug pales in comparison to what Doris Banks did.

Along with every American in August 2005, I watched the devastation of Hurricane Katrina with horror as so many lost their lives, homes, and their way of life in an instant. And like so many of us, I felt a deep desire to help. Luckily, there was a concrete way I could help people get back on their feet—I could help them find jobs.

My brother David, a filmmaker, and I packed our bags and headed to Houston. We walked into the Astrodome and I carried a sign that said, "Are you looking for a job?" Within minutes, people eager to get back to work surrounded me. I used my cell phone and BlackBerry to get in touch with their employers to claim their last paychecks. I helped them figure out how to transfer their employment to a new city.

One woman struck me with her fear and innocence. Doris was a 20-year-old single mother of a 4-year-old boy. She worked in a New Orleans Taco Bell before the hurricane and now had no idea how she was going to get out of the stadium, let alone rebuild a life for her son and herself. I decided to take her by the hand and work with her all the way.

I learned that she was eligible for rehire at any Taco Bell in Texas, so we plotted and planned to find immediate housing within walking distance of a suitable location. Then we hit the stores and bought everything to furnish this home because she had nothing but the donated clothes on her back. Doris was on the path to getting back on her feet, and I felt great that I was able to help her.

A week or so later, Lisa Belkin devoted her Sunday column in the *New York Times* to my new relationship with Doris. From that piece, I received hundreds of e-mails from readers who said that Doris was lucky to have me to help her.

Kind words, but really—Doris, lucky? The poor woman lost everything she had and suddenly found herself and her little boy in a new city with no home and no job. Doris wasn't lucky—she was smart. In the midst of a disaster, she saw an opportunity and ran to it when so many others remained on their cots and waited for help to come to them. It was her innate networking sense that got her to introduce herself to me—a total stranger—and start a relationship.

Whether it's Doris, you, or me, there's a lot of grace in asking for help. Don't be ashamed of it. And don't be stingy about giving it. More on that later.

It Takes a Network

Sandra Yancey says that five years in corporate America taught her an important lesson: Behind every successful woman is a network.

That's why Sandra founded eWomenNetwork, an organization that brings women entrepreneurs together to network, brainstorm, and achieve their goals. She is also the creator of The GLOW Project (theglowproject.org).

"Make no mistake about it: You can't climb the corporate ladder or build a multimillion dollar business by yourself," Sandra says. "Along the way, you will need to carefully cultivate a bevy of other people who will encourage you, support you, challenge you, coach you, refine you, recognize you, and cheer for you."

All things being equal—education, experience, and a passion for success—the women who come out on top are the ones who understand, invest in, and care for important relationships, Sandra says.

The best way to be successful is to become known as the one who is always helping others to be successful. "In the end, powerful people are no longer defined by their fancy titles, expensive clothes, or corner offices but by their ability to make things happen and get things done, both for themselves and others."

Never forget to say thank you all throughout your career, Sandra says. "Give without remembering and take without forgetting."

Create a Network

Let's get started on creating your network.

SIX DEGREES

It is absolutely essential to cultivate relationships with people who you perceive to be smarter, funnier, more sophisticated, and more experienced than you are. It can seem impossible to find these magical people, but they are closer than you think. Most of us have a small group of friends for personal support and enrichment. That's great. But don't rely on *The Breakfast Club* for professional advancement. Quality and quantity matter when dealing with professional relationships. Instead of having one or two people to call on when I need something for my career, I have a variety of people I reach out to, depending on the nature of my needs. Different colleagues and contacts have specific areas of expertise that I've come to count on.

In his 1973 study, "The Strength of Weak Ties," Stanford University sociologist Mark Granovetter found that weak ties—more so than strong links—led to the majority of job contacts. Earlier this year he told the *Los Angeles Times* that "when you're looking for new ideas and new connections, you don't get them from family or close friends. It's the weak ties that connect you to different circles and opportunities."

Of the people he surveyed who had secured jobs through contacts, more than 80 percent reported that they saw the contact occasionally (56 percent) or rarely (28 percent). Chance meetings and introductions by mutual friends were the most popular means of making contact.

Fill in the Six Degrees Chart on the following page by making a list of 50 people you know beyond your immediate family and very close friends. Include current and former colleagues and classmates, industry peers, the parents of your kids' friends, and so on. You'll discover that you know more people than you realize. Each name is an opportunity to reconnect, so prepare to pick up the phone or dash off an e-mail. Force yourself to fill in the entire list—now!

Six Degrees Chart

1.	26.
2.	27.
3.	28.
4.	29.
5.	30.
6.	31.
7.	32.
8.	33.
9.	34.
10.	35.
11.	36.
12.	37.
13.	38.
14.	39.
15.	40.
16.	41.
17.	42.
18.	43.
19.	44.
20.	45.
21.	46.
22.	47.
23.	48.
24.	49.
25.	50.

FOLLOW THE 60/40 RULE

Sixty percent of your job search efforts should take place off line. Forty percent should be based online. I've upped this from just 30 percent a year ago because today there's great value and connectivity online. Your time isn't limited to scouring job boards. You can make direct connections with people through online social networking.

JOIN THE PARTY

The only way to meet new people is to get out there. Go to an industry event or career fair. You'll find them listed in your industry's trade magazine, newsletter, or a major industry website. Ask co-workers and managers—current and former—where they meet new people. Go to book signings with authors writing about your field. (Barnes & Noble, Borders, Waldenbooks, and numerous independent stores have free in-store events.)

ARRIVE EARLY, STAY LATE

If you're an event rookie, you'll find it less overwhelming to walk into an event before it is packed. It will also give you an opportunity to meet people you don't know as they arrive. While you're there, participate in the planned activities. This isn't your cousin's wedding where it's okay to give the Macarena a miss. You'll seem like a team player and a good sport. Keep on your feet—you're more approachable than if you're seated. Don't just wander aimlessly. Keep your head up, make eye contact, and greet people with a firm handshake. Stay until the activities are over. You can take your cue to go when other guests are leaving, and no matter when you must depart, be sure to thank the host.

FIRM SHAKE

Indulge me for a moment on the handshake. The dead fish—that weak, floppy handshake—is the pits. I don't like half shakes either, where only the tips of your fingers touch—you're not meeting the queen. Yours should be firm without crushing your new contact.

> **Blah: Starting a conversation with "I just lost my job" and a frown.**

> **Ah!: Starting a conversation with "I'm looking for my next challenge" and a bright smile.**

INTRODUCE YOURSELF

Don't wait for the CEO of IBM to come to you. It's not going to happen. Instead, gather your courage and take the initiative to meet people. If you're shy, approach someone who is standing alone. Groups of three are often easier to join than two people chatting together. Have something in mind to talk about other than work. Watch the news before you go or read a news magazine you can discuss. Current events are perfect icebreakers.

Show Up, Make It Happen

In spring 2001 I invited Robyn Spizman, author of more than 70 books, to sign her books at my Atlanta Women For Hire career expo. She graciously spent a couple hours talking to women—and then approached me by asking if I'd like to write a book with her.

That thought had never occurred to me. As such, I told her "Of course!" I mean, who doesn't dream of being an author?

She promised to get in touch with me, but I figured I'd never hear from her again. How many times does someone put an idea on the table but never follow up? It's classic.

Not Robyn. When I got back to my office in New York there was a fax from her proposing a writing partnership and providing an introduction to her literary agent. This woman is for real, I thought.

We now have co-written four books and our most recent *Will Work from Home: Earn the Cash—Without the Commute* is a *New York Times* and *Wall Street Journal* bestseller. Robyn is one of my closest friends.

"I don't think opportunity knocks," she says. "I believe you have to show up and make it happen."

Professionally, Robyn lives by a few simple rules. She's always the first to say hello. She keeps her word. She's jump-started everything she's ever done. And she never sits on a good idea.

"I don't wait for permission," she says. "There is no permission. You don't have to raise your hand like in grade school. You have to speak up, show up, and make that extra call. We're all entitled to opportunity—if we go and create it. But it won't just show up at your door."

"WHAT DO YOU DO?"

One question that will come up often is, "What do you do?" because it's one of the main reasons people go to these events. More than likely, it will be up to you to bring up that you're out of work. Simply ask someone what he or she does, and often that person will return the question. Stay confident in yourself and in your 10- or 30-second pitch (from Chapter 2) to answer this question. Finally, don't feel embarrassed that you're unemployed—you're not the only or first person who has had to answer this question.

IT'S NOT ALL ABOUT YOU

Even if you're looking for a job, you have to bring more to the conversation than your employment status. The best way to get to know other people is by asking great questions. This can range from the basics (such as "What do you do?" "How'd you get into that line of work?" and "What brings you to this event?") to the more specific (like "What do you like to read?" and "Which teams do you follow?"). Bring some of your personality to the conversation. You want the people you meet to remember you in a distinct way.

Look for cues on name tags. When you see a company name you're familiar with, mention your connection to its products, services, or other employees.

Then you can politely segue into a request for any contacts or potential leads to be sent your way. If they agree, exchange cards and secure a time to follow up. Then move on to another subject. Discussing other topics will help you build a relationship with the people you meet and allow you to make a good, lasting impression. After about 10 minutes, it's time to meet more people. You want to meet as many contacts as possible, so don't monopolize someone's time unless it's clear that he or she wants to continue the dialogue.

Sincerity and Humility

Never undervalue the power of humility, says Mellody Hobson, president of Ariel Investments and financial contributor on *Good Morning America*: It has earned billionaire Warren Buffett the reputation as one of America's most trusted financiers.

In *The Snowball: Warren Buffett and the Business of Life*, Mellody notes that author Alice Schroeder recalled the first lesson she learned from the billionaire: "Humility disarms."

"I highlighted that passage because it's so true," Mellody says. "I'm always focused on how to demonstrate humility because it's something that's genuine, you can't fake it. When you're humble, the anxiety and judgments disappear, and you can just be who you are."

Although Buffett is a role model, Mellody says that there's a misconception about women in business—no doubt formed from popular culture in which women are often portrayed as tough, à la Meryl Streep's character in *The Devil Wears Prada*.

"I'm still surprised when people say they didn't realize I was so nice. Why wouldn't they think I'm nice?" she asks. "There's often an opinion about successful women in business that's formed before you meet them: that she's tough, aggressive, not too nice."

As such, Mellody says she strives to be extra-gracious, to take the high road.

"I work very hard to make people feel comfortable," she says. "It's important to be regular. Jargon puts distance between people. I consciously smile. I always know something about the people I'm going to meet—I read their bio so I can make a connection to find common ground."

WORKING THE ROOM

As you make your way around the room, you'll find groups already talking. Don't bust into a conversation already in progress. Walk up, listen for a few moments, and then offer a comment that does not change the subject. If the person you'd like to meet is in the middle of the conversation, don't interrupt. There will be an opening to introduce yourself if you wait for the right moment.

Once you have this person's attention, let him or her know you're looking for a new challenge, but don't bulldoze the person into promising a job or an interview. You don't want to come off desperate. Open the door to future contact by making a date to talk further and then move on.

Many women attend my Women For Hire career expos because there are 5 or even 30 different employers that they specifically want to talk to. That's great, but they're missing out on the larger opportunity if they don't introduce themselves to the other women present as well. Those other attendees tend to have great leads and resources to suggest.

> Blah: "Going to an event and hoping someone will call me."
>
> Ah!: "Picking up the phone the next morning and proactively following up on the connections I made."

HOUSE OF CARDS

Don't pass your business cards out like meaningless flyers, but be sure to have them at the ready to give to new contacts. Make a date to follow up, and note it on the back of the card you receive so that you call when you say you will. Try to make the follow-up date within 24 hours of the gathering so that you are still fresh in the contact's mind.

Follow through on any lead a networking contact gives you, even if the lead is for a job you're overqualified for and doesn't pay enough. You want that new contact to feel that you value his or her advice. And there's no downside to meeting more people and expanding your contact base.

Don't Give Up

In 2000, ABC's Bianna Golodryga was a bond trader at a Legg Mason office in Austin, Texas, where she had gone to college. She yearned to be a financial reporter on TV, but she had no television experience.

She did, however, have her broker's license, and she understood the financial markets—plusses in the world of financial news.

Yet when she applied to CNBC, the response was, "Thank you, but we're not hiring now."

"Every few weeks, I would check back in. The answer was always, 'We're still not hiring.'"

That didn't deter Bianna, who kept up her correspondence with executives there.

"I finally called and asked if I could just come in and meet them in person," she recalls. "The following day, I received a phone call saying that a spot had opened up."

She was hired as a producer on the New York Stock Exchange and stayed at CNBC for six years before joining ABC News in 2007. She reports on financial issues for *Good Morning America*.

When it comes to getting what you want in your career, Bianna says, you can't give up. "Persistence and confidence trump pride and ego."

THE RULE OF THREE

My determination to make three new contacts at every event has paid enormous dividends for my business and me, and it will for you, too. Always try to get three contacts from every event, every informational meeting, and every phone call. Get permission from the giver to use his or her name, and then do so when you make the call.

SMILE

A plain face can look like a scowl or may make you appear bored, even if it's not intended. A smile makes you approachable and shows you're happy to be wherever you are. Still . . .

IT'S NOT A FRAT PARTY

You're not at a weekend college party. This goes for an industry event, the company holiday gathering, and any situation in which you come into contact with professional peers. Check the invitation or event website for an indication of how to dress. When in doubt, dress as you would for a business meeting. Avoid alcohol—getting tipsy isn't on the agenda. And while you don't have to stuff yourself before the event to stave off hunger, you shouldn't make a pig of yourself, either. You can't shake hands with a plate in one hand and a drink in the other.

YOU MUST REMEMBER THIS

You're going to meet a lot of people when you go to these events. It is important to remember the names of these new contacts—they won't always be wearing name tags. There are tricks top executives use to fix names in their brains—use them next time you go to an event to see what works best for you.

Repeat the person's name during the initial introduction, while shaking hands. Just as with your multiplication tables in third grade, repetition is a proven memory tool.

Ask the person what he or she prefers to be called. Not only does that show interest in the person—not just the job—but it gets the person to repeat his or her name. You can also ask about the spelling or pronunciation, especially if it's unusual— anything to keep repeating the name.

Keep using the name in the conversation. Can't stress it enough: Repetition works.

Make a visual or audio connection between this new contact and someone famous or someone in your family. If the new person has hair like Albert Einstein or a voice as distinctive as your mother's, make a mental note of it.

Make a note on the person's business card to help you remember him or her after the meeting. "Jet black hair, colleague of

Jane Doe." Put these notes, and where you met the person, in your contact file.

Don't fake it. If you don't remember the person's name the next time you see him or her, just fess up. "I remember we met at the career fair. Would you please remind me of your name?" Make it clear that you remember the person, and even though his or her name slipped your mind, you want to make a connection. Better that than losing the contact altogether.

FOLLOW UP

Lest I come across as rude, I give out hundreds of cards by request to attendees at each of my career fairs. I hear from only three to five of those people within a month of the event. Maybe the rest of them didn't like me. Perhaps some lost my card. But the reality is, everyone should be following up if only with a short e-mail to thank me for my time and to remind me of a snippet from our conversation.

My friend Susan RoAne is really good at this. She ought to be because she wrote the book *How to Work a Room*. She sends me e-mails out of the blue when she sees me on TV or when she comes across an article that she thinks I'd like. Susan doesn't just call when she needs something, which is unlike many of us.

I had some fun with real estate queen Barbara Corcoran when we did a few segments together at *Good Morning America* before she jumped to NBC. She told me a great story about standing out in a crowd. When Donald Trump scored a major real estate deal, he was bombarded with obligatory notes of congratulations. Barbara sent him a note raving about the tie he wore to his big press conference, which was her way of saying, "Way to go." Every time he saw her after that, he'd thank her for recognizing that tie.

Talk about smart, memorable follow-ups.

"Remembered Me"

Wall Street Journal columnist Gwendolyn Bounds still has the stack of rejection letters from her first attempt to become a newspaper reporter. "Wallpaper material," she says.

"I'd gone the safe résumé/follow-up phone call route looking for college internships, but to no avail. I was just one of the masses," she says.

So one spring break, Wendy flew to Chicago, found the *Chicago Sun-Times* building, and sneaked right into the office where the head of human resources worked.

"He was sitting at his desk. I walked in, heart pounding, and said: 'You don't know me, but if you give me twenty seconds, you'll want to hire me.' I told him why I wanted to be an intern, handed him my résumé and a cover letter, and left before he called security."

A week later back in North Carolina, the phone rang. It was the man from the *Sun-Times*. "He remembered me and figured anyone who could get into his office unannounced might do okay in the world of journalism. I moved there a week later."

Obviously, walking in unannounced won't work in every scenario, but Wendy says it's rare that anyone gets the great job by going a traditional route.

"You don't have to 'know' someone necessarily," she says. "But you have to make yourself known to the people who are hiring in a way that sets you apart from the stacks of applicants on their desks."

As you're making those calls and sending those e-mails to the 50 people on your Six Degrees Chart, put on the Beatles' classic "Help" and REM's "Shiny Happy People" to get you into the making-contacts mood.

CHAPTER 4

Go Forth and Conquer

Anatomy of a job search—applying
and interviewing with success

Starting and growing Women For Hire has certainly not been without headaches. And some of that pain has been self-induced.

You would think that, as a producer of high-caliber career fairs, I would be an expert in recruiting my own employees. Not so. I can sum up my early days as an employer as "Workplace expert, heal thyself."

Yes, I knew how to find top-flight talent. But I struggled when it came to choosing the right people for the jobs in my shop. At first, I decided to work with people who I thought would care as much about my business as they did me—in other words, I hired my friends. We'd skip the getting-to-know-you part and get right down to work. It was a rookie mistake.

Never once did it work out. It was always a disaster. (Keep this in mind as you're looking for a job. Don't work for best friends—trust me. Help them as a favor, but think hard before signing on for a paycheck unless you've candidly explored all of the pros and cons together.)

Learning from my mistake, I decided to go in the opposite direction. I'd hire qualified people with whom I'd never want a personal relationship. It would be all work, all the time at the office. As you can imagine, that was a train wreck as well.

No Jerks Allowed

Oprah's pal Gayle King, who edits *O* magazine, says that when she is hiring what she's really looking for are people who'll fit in with her existing team.

"I don't believe that you have to like everybody you work with, but there has to be mutual respect and admiration," she told WomenForHire.com. "My preference is to work with people I like, so I look for people who are talented, accomplished in what they do, but also have a personality."

She remembers something that Shonda Rhimes, creator of *Grey's Anatomy*, said during an interview with *O*.

"She said, 'I have a no-asshole policy. I don't care how talented anybody is. I don't like to work with people who I deem assholes or difficult.'"

"That has stuck with me," Gayle said. "I like that attitude. I like that."

When I've told Women For Hire's clients—more than 1,500 ranging from IBM to the FBI—about my struggles, they laugh and say, "Welcome to our world." This is the obstacle course every employer must navigate, finding, hiring, and retaining the right people.

Most employers are looking for the perfect, ready-made package. Unfortunately, they can't browse the aisles at the Perfect Employee Emporium to find one. It's hard work. They have to find someone with the hard skills—knowledge, skills, ability—which can usually be determined by looking at a prospect's résumé.

Finding someone with the necessary soft skills is much tougher. The new employee has to be able to fit in with the existing corporate culture. Will she work well with the current employees? What makes her tick? What ticks her off?

That's what's going through an employer's mind when he or she looks at your résumé or sits across from you during an interview. You have to answer these questions and concerns for your prospective employer. Once they've decided to meet you, they have reason to believe you have the skills to do the job. At this stage, it's about the right fit. From here, camaraderie may very well trump competence.

Keep all of that in mind when you take the next step. You've gathered your courage and your contacts, zeroed in on your goals, and created a great résumé. Now it's time to start applying for jobs in an effort to land an interview.

Finding Job Leads in Every Economy

One of the huge differences between searching for a job in a strong economy and a recession lies in the difficulty of finding ample job openings. You have to shake the trees harder and dig a lot deeper to find potential leads when the economy is down.

In a healthy economy you could apply to fewer jobs and confidently assume that one would come through. But in these troubled times you'll have to search smarter to find openings and you'll have to apply for many more of them given the competition. When I appeared as a guest on *Larry King Live* to discuss the troubling job market, a caller phoned in to ask how he could possibly find a job when 90 percent of the local employers in his area said they were in a hiring freeze. That's a common question from people across the country, especially in cities where the unemployment matches or exceeds the national average. My answer is always the same: Focus on finding the other 10 percent. You don't need 100 percent of the employers to be in hiring mode. You must find just one to say yes to you.

The key to finding leads is not to rely on any single source but instead to use every avenue under the sun to unearth an opening. As you're doing so, you're not looking for a life-long commitment. Instead of focusing on security and stability, both of which are hard to guarantee even in a strong economy, look for places and opportunities that would suit you right now. College seniors often place extraordinary emphasis on launching their careers in the oh-so-perfect role. For some people that works. For others, job-searching is about exploration and curiosity—it's about trying new things and being open to possibilities.

SMALL BUSINESSES

Small businesses mainly fill jobs through word of mouth to avoid expenses of advertising. Local businesses often mention their openings to their doctors, hairdressers, storeowners, and so on. Tell your service providers that you're looking. Some small business owners post their openings on Craigslist, Facebook, or Twitter. When you're looking for a job, every conversation is an opportunity to get the word out and make a possible connection.

SOCIAL MEDIA

Not only should you post a profile on LinkedIn and Facebook, but you should also scour the job listings on those sites. You can also search discussion boards for leads on the Women For Hire group on LinkedIn. Many recruiters post openings on the boards. Update your LinkedIn, Facebook, and Twitter account profiles to reflect the type of position you're looking for. On Facebook, for example, you might update your status by saying, "Belinda is looking for an accounting position in Boston." Everyone who follows your page will have access to that information and some may respond with a lead.

> Blah: "Complaining about my job search woes on my Facebook page."
>
> Ah!: "Using Facebook to post my interest in taking on new responsibilities and exploring new challenges at my next employer."

GENERAL NETWORKING

For all the glory of the Internet and the emphasis of submitting résumés online, the reality is people hire people and your very best leads will likely come from other individuals. That means you've got to let everyone know you're looking and to ask everyone on your Six Degrees Chart (page 81) if they may be able to help you connect with an opening.

- Make early-morning and mid-afternoon visits to the Starbucks in the lobby or neighborhood of the company you're targeting. Place a tent card on your table that reads, "Please talk to me if you work for [*company name*]!"

- Ask your dentist, doctor, accountant, lawyer, hairdresser, and manicurist if any of their clients work for the companies—or in the industry—you're targeting.

- Use Twellow (twellow.com) to find people on Twitter who are involved in your industry and areas of interest.

- Research the boards of directors of charitable groups in your area, then volunteer for an organization that will enable you to connect with the executive at your target employer.

- Offer to volunteer in the speakers' lounge or during exhibit setups for conferences that will attract employees from the companies you're interested in.

- Ask 10 people you know to write a recommendation of your work on your LinkedIn.com profile. That attracts views of your profile and serves as a public recommendation.

- Call the business writer at your local newspaper to ask his or her opinion of the local companies doing the best in this economy.

- Talk to the parents of your kids' classmates. Class phone lists often reveal where those folks work.

- At your favorite shops and restaurants, chat up the sales clerks and wait staff to get the scoop on what's happening in your area.

Look for Hidden Jobs

When I kicked off the GMA Job Club in 2008—local forums where people get together to network and support one another—the idea immediately appealed to Laurie Baggett of Chesapeake, Virginia, who formed a group.

The experience has paid off for Laurie and her members.

"Since I was a child, I always dreamed about how I could help change the world," says Laurie, a human resources manager. "I believe I was born with a burning desire to make a difference. Little did I know that helping someone recognize [his or her] self-worth—and find work—does that."

In a tight economy, Laurie says, there is a "huge discrepancy between the advertised job market (where most people look) and the hidden job market, where the greatest opportunities lie."

That means that networking should be viewed as the number one job-search tool, she says.

"Even in a down economy, I help people get jobs every day," Laurie says. "I have realized that it's not just the most qualified candidates landing the jobs but the most persistent, networked, and confident."

No one can be expected to go out and sell themselves when they are "hopeless and qualified," she says. "You need to have both: qualifications for the job and hope that you will get the job."

ONLINE JOB BOARDS

You can find an abundance of opportunity on boards like Career-Builder, HotJobs, and Monster. Plug in your ZIP code and you'll find no shortage of listings. That's the good news. The bad news is that everyone else is doing the same thing. Each posting is flooded with applicants. So, although those sites are good sources for leads and ideas of who's hiring, you can't simply sit in front of your computer and apply online and expect the phone to ring.

In some ways, the big job boards offer a false sense of accomplishment. You can apply to 40 positions in one day and feel proud of yourself—surely one will pay off—but that's not how it works.

I met Shannon Joseph, a marketing executive with an MBA who relocated to Dallas with her family after Hurricane Katrina. Shannon spent her first year in her new home searching for jobs exclusively on the Internet. She submitted hundreds of résumés online in the course of that year, and I could count the number of responses she received on one hand. She has a wonderful disposition and an infectious smile, which were hidden from employers. I recommended that she move away from the computer and use other methods (like the ones described later in this chapter) to connect with employers. In no time, she had calls and interviews. Now she has a job, too.

MORE PLACES TO FIND LEADS

Here are some of the other places to look for leads.

The Sunday Paper

Yes, the old-fashioned way of looking in your Sunday newspaper still works, even though the help-wanted section is thinner than ever before. It features legitimate opportunities—employers are paying weekly to advertise in that space—and because the number of people who actually read a newspaper is decreasing, you may not face as much competition as you do with online ads.

Trade Publications

Every major industry now publishes a print or electronic magazine or newsletter, which often contains job postings. For example, the National Retail Federation (nrf.com) publishes a daily e-newsletter on the latest industry headlines. It features a section with job openings in the field.

Career Fairs

Look at the Sunday paper for ads for career or job fairs and google the terms *career fair* and *job fair* to find events in your area. If you are able to attend a fair, keep the following in mind:

- *Do your homework*. Scour the career fair's website for information about the companies that will be there. Find out more about those organizations by going to their websites (while you're there, find out about what jobs are open). Go to Hoovers (hoovers.com) for an independent profile of the companies' strengths, weaknesses, and competitors. On the fair's website, check for seminars, special guests, and other perks, such as résumé critiquing.

- *Rise and shine.* Get a good night's sleep and eat a good breakfast before you get to the fair—and get there early. You'll get more face time with a fresher recruiter if you get there before the crowds.

- *Dress the part.* Business attire that pops is a must. Go for comfortable business shoes. After a day on your feet, you'll thank me. Another tip: Check your coat. You don't want to be weighed down, and you want to present a fresh, crisp appearance. Add color to your wardrobe to stand out.

- *Come armed and ready.* Have a stack of focused résumés and crisp business cards ready to hand out. Bring a bag to hold all the company literature you'll pick up. Have a notebook to take notes about follow-ups.

- *Case the joint.* Get your bearings as you walk through the hall; pick up as much literature as you can from companies that interest you. It's smart to start at the back, where there are representatives waiting for someone to appear.

- *Meet and greet.* Watch closely as others talk to the recruiter to get a sense of the kind of person you'll be meeting and how he or she conducts the converstion. Be prepared to succinctly explain how you meet the company's needs. Ask how you can follow up (such as a phone call or email) and what the procedure is. And get the recruiter's business card so you can make that connection. If no card is forthcoming, be sure to jot down the name of the recruiter; you'll see it on his or her name tag. You can always go to the company site to get a main number to track down that person.

■ *Talk to other job hunters*. Fellow job hunters are valuable contacts, too. Maybe they've been to company booths that you've missed, know of other resources you can use, or can brainstorm with you on how to cover more ground. Don't view them as competitors; they're actually comrades in training to find great work, just like you. You can learn from one another.

Blah: "I've got to elbow other job seekers out of the way to get face time with the recruiter."

Ah!: "I can share information with others at the fair to get—and give—more from the experience."

Government Listings

Career One Stop operates its own job bank and is definitely worth a visit to its website: careeronestop.gov

Staffing Firms

Register with local staffing agencies in your geographic area and search online for firms that specialize in your industry, regardless of their location. For example, a national nonprofit staffing firm located in New York might have listings for jobs in cities throughout the northeast.

Before you sign on with a staffing firm, ask your contact some questions:

- What types of clients do you have?

- What is your firm's specialty?

- How much repeat business do you have from your clients?

- What is your placement rate?

- How do you determine which candidates are sent on interviews?

When sending you out on an interview, the firm should be able to give you as much information as possible so that you're completely prepared. You should also be kept up to date on the jobs your résumé is being submitted for. If the firm isn't doing those two key things, and if it charges a fee, look for another agency.

But what's really important is that you keep searching on your own. You can't rely on a staffing firm to get you a job. You have to keep hitting all your resources.

Professional Associations

As a member of a group in your industry you may have access to job listings on a website or via e-mail. If no formal job bank exists, inquire about how job leads are shared with members.

Career Services

If you're still in school, which includes adult learning programs, make an appointment with the school's career services office. Find out which employers recruit from your program, how to connect with alumni working in your field of interest, and how to have access to job openings submitted to your school. If you've long since graduated, contact the alumni relations department to ask about job search assistance.

Applying for a Job

When you see a job posting that sounds appealing, it's time to apply. And this takes some serious skill.

Gone are the days of simply mailing your resume, receiving a call, shaking hands at the interview, and agreeing on a start date. The Internet has taken over the recruiting landscape, and everyone is required to submit a résumé online. While that brings greater efficiency to the process for employers, it can be awfully maddening for job seekers. But it doesn't have to be that way if you know how to navigate the system.

Consider these straightforward steps before pressing the SUBMIT button:

1. Print out the job posting that you're interested in pursuing before you apply.

2. Use a highlighter to mark the keywords and industry language used to describe the requirements and responsibilities of that role.

3. Compare those words and phrases to the language that appears on your current résumé.

4. Figure out how and where to add the most relevant keywords to your résumé, assuming you have the specific knowledge, skills, and experience. Sophisticated applicant tracking systems search for keyword matches; the more matches, the better, which often determines if a recruiter opts to view your résumé.

5. Once you're confident that your résumé reflects a strong match, go ahead and submit that targeted résumé online.

6. Don't overapply. Submit your résumé for no more than three positions at any company. Many people are so gung-ho on getting into an organization that they apply to 15 openings, assuming one will lead to a call. Instead, the system flags (and disqualifies) all of them because nobody is an ideal match for that many roles. It makes you look desperate, not determined.

7. If the system requests a cover letter, write a short one that expresses why you're a strong match and why you'd like to join the organization. This extra step is often overlooked. I know it's extra work, but it's worth it because it offers you a chance to tout the research you've done on the role and the employer.

8. Never submit a generic, one-size-fits-all résumé or cover letter. If you really want the position, you'll customize both documents for each job.

9. Once you apply, get to work to find an internal referral to make a personal introduction. Here's how:

■ Refer back to your list of 50 people you know (page 81) and ask each one of those individuals if he or she knows someone who works (or has worked) for that employer.

■ Attend job fairs to meet face-to-face with employers and other professionals.

■ Create a free profile and become active on LinkedIn (see Chapter 3). Surely you can find someone who knows someone to help make that connection.

- Join an association in your field, and network with like-minded peers. Access the member directory to find a connection to the company.

- Connect with your high school and college alumni groups. Old pals could be new connectors.

- Talk to your unlikely network. For example, look at the class list of the parents of your kids' friends. Anytime my kids hear about a friend's mom or dad who's lost a job, they tell them to call me. Even though we don't know each other, we have a common connection, which can sometimes lead to a contact.

10. Follow up with a call or e-mail within two days to the recruiter responsible for filling the position. Never say, "Did you get my résumé?" Instead be ready to reiterate your strong qualifications and interest in the role. You'll have just a brief moment to sell yourself, so rehearse before making the call or sending the e-mail. Try to get someone on the phone directly instead of leaving a voicemail message. This may require a few attempts, so vary the times of day you place the calls. Ultimately, someone will pick up.

11. Don't know the name of the right person? Cold-call the company and ask an operator to put you through. If that doesn't work, google the term *recruiter* or *HR director* along with the name of your employer of choice. The results may reveal the name you're trying to find. LinkedIn is another resource for finding contact names.

12. Stay fresh in the recruiter's mind. Every recruiter is different, which makes this a challenge. Some say you're welcome to follow up weekly. Others say every other week is enough.

And then there are some who'll tell you to never call. Find the right balance so you're politely persistent without crossing over to a pest. If you're unsure, ask.

13. Ask directly for advice on how and when to follow up. A simple question, "What's the best way to keep in touch?" will give you the details you need to stay ahead of the pack.

A couple other options, while not essential, may be used to further your candidacy:

- Mail a copy of your résumé with a targeted cover letter and even a copy of the job posting *in addition to,* not instead of, the online submission to the HR department.

- Identify the head of the department you'd be working for (this is where LinkedIn or cold calling can come in handy) and send that person a letter introducing yourself and noting your keen interest in the position.

INTERVIEW PREP

They want you. Or at least, they want to meet with you. So far, so good. This is a great opportunity, so don't blow it. Time to prep for your grilling.

Always Prepare

Before Elissa Ellis Sangster became executive director of the Forté Foundation, a consortium of major corporations and top business schools, she ran MBA programs at Texas A&M University and the University of Texas.

"As a natural extrovert, I have a tendency to wing it when standing up in front of an audience," she says. "I had made it through most of my career because my audience was somewhat forgiving: students who knew me well and work colleagues."

But when she assumed her duties at Forté, which included speaking at many conferences and corporate meetings, that old style seemed, well, old.

"I wasn't proud of my performance. I tried my old way a couple of times, but didn't like the outcome or the way I felt during the presentation," Elissa recalls.

So she got to work. She began writing her speaking notes down beforehand to give herself a better idea of what she wanted to communicate. She would rehearse her presentations out loud.

"The more I prepared and rehearsed, the more polished my presentations became," she says. "This approach is really a good one, whether you're afraid of public speaking or are just concerned with communicating in the most effective way possible. If you're well prepared, you'll be more confident, and your speaking engagements will be much more successful."

Pass the Phone Screen

You got the callback, but there's usually one more step before you get your foot in the door: the phone screen. Today, just about every recruiter opts to talk with prospective candidates by phone before scheduling an in-person interview. Treat this conversation as seriously as you would if you were face-to-face. Blow this call, and the opportunity will end when the recruiter hangs up the phone.

When you're ready to pick up the phone, turn off all background noises. Try to make the call from a landline, not a cell phone. If you must use a cell phone, be sure there's a clear connection and stand in one place. I've gotten calls from candidates as they walk down the street. Never a good thing. Don't multitask; this call is the only thing you should be focusing on for the moment.

Rehearse what you're going to say. Every time I receive an inquiry from an applicant, the person is stunned if I get on the phone. She expected to speak to an assistant. Be ready for both scenarios—an assistant and the recruiter or hiring manager. This will prevent you from being caught off guard.

To an assistant, you'll introduce yourself, reference the position you've applied for, and ask for directions for how to call attention to your interest. For example, "Hi, my name is Sophie Smith. I recently applied for the marketing position on your website, and I'm an ideal match for the role. I was hoping I might be able to talk to the recruiter responsible for filling the role or perhaps you might be willing to offer me some guidance on how to get my foot in the door for an interview." Be sure to get the name of the person you speak with and have a pen handy to take notes on any direction he or she offers.

If you get the recruiter directly, you'll tweak that slightly. "Hi, this is Sophie Smith, and I recently applied for the marketing position on your website. I've studied the job posting, and I'm an ideal match for that role, so I wanted to call to introduce myself directly to you, especially because I'm sure you're getting lots of interest." You should quickly reference where you've worked and why you are a perfect match for the job.

Even though you can rehearse, you must also be ready for the unexpected. You may be invited to talk longer than you expected or your call could be cut short. Anything can happen. If you're smiling, poised, and confident, you'll handle it with ease.

One of the big pitfalls to avoid is using *um, uh, ya know, like, um, ah, ya know.* Usually we use these fillers without even realizing it. If you're prone to this, especially when you're nervous, write down the words on a sheet of paper in front of you when you make the call. When you catch yourself about to say one, pause. It's perfectly acceptable to take a breath and pause for a second or two; you don't have to talk nonstop, making every other word an empty filler.

Aim High and Be Confident in Yourself

When talking to women about their careers, I often hear examples of self-doubt, ranging from "Nobody would ever take me seriously in that position, so I won't even apply," to "They'll never pay me more money, so I won't even ask."

A winning attitude can open doors others tell you are closed (more on that in a minute), and telling yourself that you can't get what you want is a fait accompli. Nothing ventured, nothing gained . . . I've got plenty of clichés for this one. The bottom line: No one's going to give you what you want unless you step up and ask for it. No Little Miss (or Mister) Naysayer here, please!

I'm reminded of Michael Gelman, the executive producer of *Live with Regis and Kelly*, whom I interviewed for my second book, *Women For Hire's Get-Ahead Guide to Career Success*. He recalled his college years when he asked professors for advice on how to land a job in TV. All of them suggested pounding the pavement in small markets, even offering to work for free. But he had other, bigger plans.

Gelman told me that he figured that someone had to get those big-city TV jobs, so why not him? That attitude and perseverance landed him a coveted spot on Regis Philbin's popular daytime talk show, *Live,* and in just a few years, Gelman rose through the ranks to be named executive producer—one of the few in TV with an on-air presence.

So tap into your inner Gelman and go for it!

Dress the Part

It's important to know the culture of the environment in which you want to work. It might be okay to wear jeans to an interview at Starbucks, but not to a Fortune 500 company. Okay, that's pretty obvious, but company culture is not always that clear cut. How you present yourself has a direct correlation to how you're perceived. If you want respect on the job, you have to present yourself in a way that shows you respect the position. If you don't know the dress code before going into an interview, ask the HR executive arranging the meeting or ingratiate yourself to the boss's assistant to get that inside scoop. And if you want to start climbing the ladder at your present job, take a good look in the mirror to see what your appearance is saying about your attitude. It may be time for an adjustment.

Details Count

You could have the classiest business suit on, but if your hair is a mess, you're drenched with perfume or cologne, and you're chewing gum, forget it. The impression is that you ran out and bought that suit when you got the interview but you really have no idea how you're perceived. Would you want someone like that to represent *your* company? Of course not.

Standing Out.

We've seen headline-grabbing tactics—the guy who takes to the streets with "hire me" sandwich boards or the woman who buys a billboard to advertise her availability to drivers on a crowded highway. They rarely work but some gimmicks can even backfire.

One recruiter in financial services told me she was close to extending an offer to a candidate for an accounting position until he arranged for a clown to show up at her office with a note. It read, "Filling this position is no laughing matter, so don't clown around. Hire me because I can juggle the demands with ease." Clever, but the timing couldn't be worse. Just two hours earlier, she had learned of a death in her family. She said the accounting role required someone to use proper judgment, not bozo moves. Be very, very sure of your audience before you pull a stunt.

Do Your Homework, Part 1

I heard a story about a writer interviewing for a job at *Good Morning America* who said, without blinking, that he didn't watch *GMA* or any morning show, couldn't name the anchors and had no idea who ran the show. Seriously. He thought his résumé was enough to get the job. Not only did his cavalier attitude insult the interviewer but his manner said, in no uncertain terms, that he didn't even know—or care—what *GMA*'s mission was each morning.

This is an extreme example, but the point holds true. I always ask applicants what they know about my company in interviews. Half the time they can't answer, or they say they thought we'd discuss it together, or they just plain get it wrong. What that tells me is that those interviewees, while impressive on paper, didn't care enough about the meeting to do any digging. The conversation ends there.

Before you walk into the meeting, learn everything you can about the company. Here are the questions you should have answers to before walking in:

- Number of employees (Is it 5 or 5,000?)

- Nature of the products or services offered (Is it software or casual wear?)

- Target market (Who are the customers and clients?)

- General company history (Is it a start-up or Fortune 500?)

- Competitors (Think Coke vs. Pepsi.)

- Specifics about the departments your position would serve (What are their profitabilities? Where are they located?)

- Recent news about the company (Think earnings to expansion and layoffs to liabilities.)

- Corporate culture (Are they casual Fridays or 12-hour days?)

How do you find all that information? Go to the company's website and read it link by link. Everything from the products the company sells, the number of employees, the number and locations of branch offices, the executive biographies, the plans for the company picnic, read all of it. Go to the press or media links to find out what the company is telling the outside world about itself. Especially check out the job links, even for positions that aren't for you. Reading the application information may reveal something about company requirements or indicate that a particular division is growing.

To find out what the outside world has to say about the company, search for it in Google News to see if it has been in the headlines lately. There are also sites such as Hoovers, Vault, and WetFeet that provide extensive information on companies and industries. For an executive look at the business world, go to CEOExpress. You should also look at how the company's doing in the market. Just type in the company's name on Yahoo! and you'll retrieve a profile, stock prices, and recent news on the industry.

Read industry trade papers, talk to someone who works there

and to a competitor to get the inside scoop—anything you can think of to walk in knowing you've done everything you can to be informed. You'll feel more confident, and it will show.

Do Your Homework, Part 2

After I was fired from NBC, a friend set me up for an interview as a publicist at ABC's *Primetime Live,* which meant I would be meeting with anchor Diane Sawyer.

I went to that meeting loaded for bear—a file bursting with my press clippings and an agenda of what I wanted to discuss. I was ready. Or so I thought.

Diane didn't look at my file. She didn't ask me about my experience in PR. She assumed that if I got my foot in her door, I could do PR. What she didn't know was who I was and what made me tick. Her first question for me: "What do you read?" I panicked. Was it a trick question? Was she going to grill me about the *New York Times* headlines or latest *New Yorker* cover story? Needless to say, I didn't get the job. Years later, when we worked together, at *Good Morning America* she told me that she hires based on curiosity.

That experience gave birth to a question I always ask in interviews: "How do you keep up with current events?" I actually get answers like, "I'm not that into the news," or "My parents (spouse, friends) call me when something big happens." If you think this makes you sound like you're so devoted to your field that you don't have time for anything else, you're wrong. It makes you sound disconnected to the world around you. Employers want educated, interested, and engaged employees.

Follow the headlines—in the world, your community, and your industry. Know what's happening. Some of the best ideas come from applying what's going on outside your work to your field. (In the Resources section I recommend several websites to bookmark to help you keep up on the latest news.)

Blah: "I don't have time to read the paper every day."

Ah!: "I must make time to read the daily paper because keeping up with local and world events enables me to have smart conversations with everyone I encounter. Plus I feel smarter and more confident when I know what's happening around me."

Know Thy Interviewer

Don't just research the company, get some information on the individuals you'll be meeting with. Google them and search for their names on LinkedIn, Facebook, and on the company website. If you made the contact through a friend or colleague, find out everything you can from your pal. If the interviewer has a common name (like Jones), you can ask if she is the same Thea Jones quoted in a recent *Los Angeles Times* article (thank you, Google). If she is, great. If she isn't, it's still impressive that you went to the trouble to find out more about her. You can look on the company website or ask the HR department for a bio of the person you'll be meeting.

DURING THE INTERVIEW

Be Enthusiastic

This is Part Two of the Gelman recipe for success. This is not the time to be modest or demure. You have to present an assured, winning attitude without coming off like a blowhard, and you need to do this verbally and nonverbally. Verbally, you don't want to sound wimpy, whiny, loud, or hyper. Express your desire in an energetic but not over-the-top way. Nonverbally, greet the interviewer with a firm handshake, not a bone crusher and not a dead fish. Smile, sit up straight, make eye contact, and speak from a position of strength. Genuine confidence and enthusiasm are contagious. If an employer sees that in you, then he or she is going to feel confident and enthusiastic about you as well.

The opening moments of the interview are a good time to mention that *LA Times* article or some connection to the interviewer. It's not about sucking up, it's about creating an atmosphere conducive to conversation. Most likely, the interviewer will do that, but be prepared just in case.

Be Ambitious, but Be Yourself

As a child growing up in a modest household in Perry, Georgia, ABC News correspondent Deborah Roberts was taught that ambition and aggressiveness were no-no's. That held her back during her early years in TV news, she says.

"I saw other people get assignments that they perhaps weren't as qualified for as I was, but because they spoke up and went after it, it was theirs to have," she says. "It wasn't until I started speaking up did I gain the confidence that I needed to get the assignments I wanted."

In retrospect, Deborah says she learned that "being aggressive doesn't have to mean being a barracuda or a shark. I can still be myself and be comfortable with who I am—but also be ambitious and aggressive. You can be hard charging in a good way."

She recalls something that ABC's Barbara Walters—a trailblazing TV newswoman—taught her early on at ABC's newsmagazine *20/20*.

"I had notes in front of me of what I thought I was expected to say, and Barbara yanked my notes and said, 'Just be yourself.' She reminded me that I knew the report and the material better than anyone and told me to just be me. At that moment I hit a different zone. I had a confidence level that led to better work, people started commenting on how well I was doing, and I got better assignments."

Blah to *Ah!*: What's on Your Feet and in Your Mouth?

Unless you have a ballerina's posture, avoid flats during interviews and important meetings. Wear heels; not the ones that belong exclusively in a nightclub, but the ones that make you stand tall and appear confident. Pop a breath mint—I always do before a speech, an important meeting, or even a TV segment. I don't do it because I'm afraid my breath stinks. It's a confidence booster. No chipped nail polish. Having polished shoes and carrying a good bag will give you that extra sense of security as well. Guys, looks count for you, too. Get those shoes shined—and since you can't get sneakers shined, they're out. Your suit and shirt must be pressed and your tie spot-free. Button your shirt's top button and make sure your Windsor knot is tied correctly. All the extra stuff that you carry in your pockets—from a pack of gum to your wallet to your Game Boy—should be tucked into your briefcase, not your back pocket, to give you a sharp look. The only thing you need close at hand is a case for those mint-condition business cards.

Don't Overshare

Desperate times often lead people to say things they later regret. Everyone has a personal story about how the recession is affecting them. Keep that to yourself. Don't divulge the troubles making mortgage payments or the arguments with creditors. If your family is on your case about "finally" finding work, stay mum. Prevent the interviewer from getting a glimpse at your baggage. Keep the conversation professional.

Answering Questions

Although all interviews are different, there are several common questions you can expect about your knowledge, experience, and skills. Preparation and confidence are the keys to acing the interview. Practice answering and asking these types of questions with a friend or in front of the mirror. You'll feel much more at ease when you walk in. Most interviewers will throw in a zinger, so be prepared for the questions you can anticipate and face the zinger if and when it comes.

Let's look at some common interview questions.

Tell Me about Yourself

You can expect to be asked to talk about yourself. Yes, it's wide open, which is a gift, because that means you can maneuver your answer anyway you like. A good mixture of personal and professional works well here, but make sure it relates directly to the company. If you're interviewing at Weight Watchers, you can mention that you'd like to drop a few pounds. That tidbit won't work well at Hershey's. However, you might tell the folks at Hershey how you grew up watching Mom whip up great desserts that your family loved, so much so that you want to be part of a company that helps create those memories for other families.

Why Are You out of Work? How Do You Spend Your Time?

I'd put money on your being asked about being out of work. If you were part of a large layoff or your department was eliminated, say so. This takes the stigma of being out of work off you and puts it on the economy. If your unemployment is your own fault (you were fired or quit), be honest but choose your words carefully. Quitting a job without another lined up doesn't look good unless you can explain why you opted to blithely go without a paycheck.

Simply saying, "There was no room for growth" won't cut it in this climate. Even if you were escaping a bad boss, you should try to shift it to something personal—choosing to take classes, to care for a relative, or even to devote proper time to an effective job search to change direction in your career.

If you were fired for cause, rehearse your answer and keep it brief. It's okay if you didn't get along with a boss or made a mistake because not every situation works out. Just accept responsibility in your *short* explanation and move on.

Be ready to explain how you've spent your time if you've been out for more than three months. If you say your job search takes 24/7, then it begs the question why you haven't yet been hired. Focus on something positive. You might say, this is the first time you've been out of work in 10 years. While your top priority is to secure the right position, you've also used the time to reconnect with colleagues, take a class, start a blog on this industry, care for your mother, or whatever the truth is.

Feel free to take notes during an interview, especially if you're concerned about remembering key points for follow-up. And on a related note: cell phones and Blackberries should be turned off during a job interview.

Free at Last

Carly Fiorina went through one of the most public firings when Hewlett-Packard removed her as its chair and CEO in 2005.

"It was traumatic," she told WomenForHire.com. "I certainly had some rough days and sleepless nights after that."

"It was unexpected. It was dramatic. It played out in the media. People I trusted in many ways betrayed me. And yet, there was a gift in that. One of those gifts was I realized I wasn't afraid of anything anymore. And, I don't feel I have anything to prove anymore. I'm very proud of my accomplishments there. I think I made a big difference for that company."

What's Your Greatest Strength?

When an interviewer asks about your strengths, he or she really means, "Do you have what it takes to excel at this company?" The answer should focus on how you can succeed in the position you're going for. If the job is in customer service, you'd say that one of your greatest strengths is in problem solving, and give an example of how you've succeeded in this capacity in the past. Review the job postings 24 hours before the interview so your memory is refreshed on what the employer is looking for. Come up with three examples of how your work history—and your successes—mesh with what the company seeks.

What's Your Greatest Weakness?

A potential land mine is being asked about your weaknesses. Be honest, but not too honest. Think of it this way: Two people can have a pleasant first date, a fine time over a meal, a good chat at a cocktail party. But that doesn't mean they revealed their real selves. Chances are you worked hard to put on a happy face and present your best self. Anyone can make a good impression in 15 minutes.

The responsibility of the interviewer is to get you to let your hair down—to scratch beneath the surface, to peel back the layers. In other words, to get to know the real you.

Asking about your weaknesses is one way to ask what's wrong with you. Resist the urge to mask a strength as a weakness. ("I have a tendency to work too hard." If you think that's a weakness, I definitely won't hire you.)

Because you should reveal something that's honest and genuine about yourself, I can't tell you exactly what to say. I can only offer you a few examples.

Sample 1: "In an effort to maintain full control over projects from start to finish, I resisted the urge to delegate. On more than one occasion, I realized that I couldn't do it all on my own, and I needed the help of others. I've consciously worked on assigning tasks and working effectively with a team to deliver success. Ultimately, the result is stronger than what I could have done on my own."

Sample 2: "Even though I've never missed a deadline, I would typically wait until the eleventh hour to complete an assignment. For example, when I had three months to do something, I'd wait until I had just three or four weeks to go. While the quality of my work was always complimented, the self-induced stress was getting to me. I've since stuck to timelines that allow me to pace myself, making valuable use of all the allotted time. It feels better to avoid the mad rush, and it's something I continue to monitor to make sure I'm consistently on task."

Sample 3: "I've always struggled with organization. I would joke that I thrive among organized chaos. Things may look a mess, and my desk may not be the neatest, but I know what's what. Yet when my Outlook inbox hit a thousand messages, it occurred to me that I might do better by creating some system. I researched best practices online, and now I've mastered it. My desk still won't win any awards for spotlessness, but I never have more than a dozen or so messages at any one time in my inbox."

Sample 4: "Public speaking terrifies me. I'm confident in my work and I know my industry very well. I can write strong documents, and I'm perfectly comfortable speaking one on one or in small groups. But if you force me to present in front of a hundred people, my palms sweat, and my knees buckle. As my career advances, I recognize the importance both personally and professionally of overcoming this weakness. I recently learned of a Toastmasters group and I'm reading a Dale Carnegie book, both of which will help me lick the fear."

Where Do You See Yourself in Five Years?

Interviewers love to ask you about your short-term future. It's tricky. If you approach it as a go-getter and respond, "I want your job," some people will love your chutzpah; others will think you're obnoxious. On the other hand, if you answer, "I'm really focused on leaping into this job and learning all I can about the business," some interviewers will think you have no drive or vision. My advice: Prepare two truthful answers, and read the room. Usually you can tell what the boss is looking to hear. You can never go wrong by expressing a desire to grow with the company. You don't have to say how or where. You get the idea.

Other topics that might surface during an interview include the following:

- *Your last boss or position*. As I recommend in Chapter 1, you must be positive when discussing either your last boss or position, even if both leave a bad taste in your mouth.

- *What your former boss would say about you*. Here's where you focus on the best and leave out the worst. This is a good time to share your accomplishments: "She was pleased that I was able to double our sales in the second quarter of 2008."

- *Why are you the right person for this job?* The answer is not, "I need the money" or "It's close to my home." The answer is about how much you'll enjoy doing the work and succeeding at it. The same goes with questions like, "Why is this job appealing to you?" This too is a question you can rehearse at home by studying the job posting before your interview. What excites you about the role? Why are you thrilled to be interviewing for it? If this is a position as a nursery-school teacher, you can talk about your love of learning and the satisfaction you get from helping to mold young minds. Refer to the curriculum and the school's reputation and how proud you'd be to continue its rich history. If the role is a marketing manager for a start-up, you can reference your marketing skills and successes as well as your keen interest in contributing to the successes of building a business from the ground up.

If you can answer these types of questions with concrete answers, you will show yourself to be confident, self-aware, and driven to succeed for that company. Just writing the answers out will boost your confidence. Go back and reread your answers when you feel your confidence lagging.

Just Get out There

Planned Parenthood president Cecile Richards says that the best career advice she always got was from her mom, the late Texas Governor Ann Richards.

"She always said that failing is not a bad thing and that in fact some of the best lessons she learned were from her failures, not her successes," Cecile told WomenForHire.com.

Her mom always encouraged her to take a chance, "even if you don't know you're going to be successful because at the end of the day, you're going to grow out of that experience."

"Here was a young woman who came out of Waco, Texas, who had everything happen to her that could happen that you could say would be an excuse for her not making it—her marriage ended, she was an alcoholic, she lost a really tough gubernatorial race—and from each of those experiences she just came back at it."

Her mother was the ultimate role model for women: she showed them "what they can do when they put their minds to it, to not listen to all those tapes in their heads about why they're not good enough. Her message was: 'Just get out there and do it.'"

Asking Questions

You get a turn to ask questions too, so make the most of it. Don't cede all the control to the other side. Even though the interview process requires you to sell yourself to the employer, they're not the only ones with decision-making power. Just as they're evaluating you, you must determine whether you'd be happy with them.

Here are a few examples:

- How did you come to the company? (Everyone loves talking about himself or herself.)

- What's your management style?

- I understand the primary duties with this position. What are some of the secondary responsibilities? How often are they required?

- What are some of the challenges facing the department in the next 90 days?

■ Why is this position vacant? (Maybe the previous employee was promoted, which means that someone has been successful in the position and the company likes to promote from within.)

■ What are the qualifications of previous employees who've excelled at this position? (See what you can learn from and about predecessors in this role.)

■ What are the company's growth plans? (This gives you a sense of the future.)

■ If there is something you could change about the culture of the team or department, what would it be? (This is as close as you can get to asking, "What's wrong with this place?" without being rude.)

■ What are the next steps in this process? (Never leave the interview without establishing the time frame and specific steps for following up. When might you expect to hear from the company? Will you be required to meet with other people? Is there any testing involved? When does the company expect to make a decision? You can go so far as to establish when you should contact the interviewer and by what means, such as phone or e-mail, if you don't hear back as expected.)

The responses to these questions may strengthen your interest in the role or could cause you to flee from the opportunity. Just don't give up your power in the process. And at the end of the day, never ignore your intuition. That voice in the back of your head will make noise if something doesn't feel right about the opportunity. Pay attention to all cues and continue to probe and follow up until you're satisfied that you have all of the information and answers that you need.

Be Choosy About Where You Work

In a difficult economy, telling people to be choosy about what jobs they accept might be a difficult concept to swallow.

Yet that's what digital marketing executive Marisa Thalberg recommends, because she's been there.

Several years ago she accepted a position as head of marketing for a midsize home-furnishings company, leaving behind her post at a high-profile beauty company.

She felt good about the move because she was nervous about the long-term health of her former employer, and her new CEO tempted her with the potential for big financial payoff down the road.

But "from the moment I got there, I felt like a fish out of water," she says. "It was hard to muster that same enthusiasm when the environment was so much less stimulating and right for me."

This hard lesson came with a second punch: Not only was the company not headed for endless growth but it wound up in Chapter 11.

"In accepting a job, you have to consider the environment and culture fit as much as the work itself," Marisa says. "If you find yourself intellectualizing why a potential position would be good for you, even if your heart and gut are railing against it, that's a pretty significant warning sign worth heeding. Once you cross the finish line to finding a new job, you're really just starting a whole new marathon of thriving within it."

Interviewing While Pregnant

Every pregnant woman wonders if she should tell a prospective employer that she's pregnant. It's a tough one. It's illegal for an interviewer to ask about your pregnancy, although, if you're showing no one needs to ask. (An interviewer can ask if the pregnancy will affect your ability to do the job, such as a package-delivery person or an x-ray technician.)

Showing or not, you should always be prepared to answer the question. Whether you offer the information depends on the situation.

Not showing: Wait until you get the offer before you bring it up. Keep the focus on why you can do the job, not why you'll have to take time off after you get it. Just knowing that they may lose a new employee for a month or three will give even the most open-minded employer a subconscious reason not to give you the job. Once you get and accept a firm offer, discuss your expectations and intentions for maternity leave.

Showing: If you're well into your pregnancy, you should be prepared to address it by confidently focusing on your unique experience, skill set, and ability to perform the requirements of the position. Be clear about your intentions to take a normal maternity leave and assure the interviewer that you are ready to blend both work and family effectively.

Keep in mind that the biggest concern an employer has when interviewing anyone—pregnant or not—is your ability to do the job effectively.

AFTER THE INTERVIEW

Follow Up with a Thank-You

Always follow up an interview by e-mail within 24 hours. If you really want to impress, send an additional handwritten note. The follow-up isn't just a chance to reiterate your interests and strengths, it's also an opportunity to retract mistakes, if any. Once again, don't be general. Be specific and reflect comments or concerns articulated in the interview. If the decision maker focused heavily on the need for the successful candidate to excel in a specific area, this is the time and place to reiterate your skill level. Let the recipient know you were paying attention to all of his or her concerns. If you met with more than one person, each should receive a customized note. Don't send group thank-yous.

What If You Mess Up?

Not too long ago I met a lovely mother who was out of work and struggling to provide for her two teens. I was eager to help her get back on her feet.

She expressed an interest in healthcare administration, so I set her up on an interview for an administrative job at one of the most prestigious cancer-care hospitals in the world. We practiced how she would answer questions about being an older woman out of work and how she should approach the interview with energy and confidence. She felt well prepared for the interview.

Then I got some honest feedback from the internal recruiter. It was tough to hear.

When asked what she was doing to find work, my pal answered, "Sitting and waiting for something to come along." She told the interviewer that she volunteers on her co-op board and at her son's school. How does that help you with your job search, she was asked. "Well, it just keeps me busy to pass the time."

Wrong and wrong.

She was then asked for an example of a mistake she had made. The response: "Sometimes I make a move without thinking through the impact of the decision fully," and gave as an example, "I once left a job without another one lined up. I didn't know it would take so long to find work."

Wrong again. It was as if all the preparation fled from her brain.

The recruiter told me that because of her questionable judgment and lack of initiative, the medical center was not interested in hiring her.

I relayed this feedback, and the mom burst into tears, denying it all. In an effort to turn things around, I helped her write the thank-you note below to correct the mistakes she made in the interview.

Dear [Interviewer]:

Just a note to thank you so much for your time today. I'm thrilled to have performed well on the skills assessments, which I trust speaks to my administrative abilities.

I also reflected on a few of the things we discussed, and I'd appreciate the chance to clarify something. In my desire to be exceptionally candid with you, I hope I didn't downplay all that I'm doing every day to secure a new position. I focus proactively on my search every day. From networking with the board in my building to volunteering at my son's school to attending professional events, I'm reaching out to new people and nurturing relationships daily. I'm also in touch with multiple agencies, where I've tested well and am at the top of the lists for placement once positions open. I submit résumés online and follow up each day with many of those submissions. But at some point, my hands are tied—and I must wait for the process to take its natural progression. That's not, however, to say that I'm sitting around and waiting; it's that I have many sticks in the fire, and I know one will catch soon!

I'd like nothing more than for that one to be at your medical center. While I may not be the best job seeker or the best interviewee, I have always performed exceptionally well while at work. Being unemployed is so foreign and uncomfortable to me. I love being accountable and on the job. I've always exhibited great judgment for my co-workers, clients, and employers.

I'm confident if given the opportunity, I'd serve the whole hospital community quite well. My friend [name], who has worked there for 12 years, will tell you that my personality and professionalism are of the caliber your patients, doctors, and administrators expect.

Thank you very much for your time and consideration.

Best regards,

[Her name]

Yes, it would have been much better if she had done well face-to-face, but addressing her errors in the thank-you note showed strength, candor, and a take-charge attitude. She was given another chance to continue the interview process.

Bridging the Financial Gap

In an ideal world, you'd pursue only a position that you'd love waking up to every day and one that you'd dream of keeping for years to come. But, unfortunately, things aren't picture perfect right now. Not everyone can work for free until a position becomes available. That often means taking a job—any job—just to bring in a paycheck.

If you're busting your butt to support yourself, I'm not a fan of labeling it "settling." To me, settling is racking up debt, depleting your savings, and waiting idly for something to eventually come along.

Blah: "Taking any old survival job, without giving much thought to my more serious long-term career goals."

Ah!: "Aligning my long-term sights with my short-term options." (For example, you may be looking to join an interior design firm, but in the interim you'd like a retail survival job. Consider Crate & Barrel, Home Depot Expo Design Center, or a high-end antiques or boutique shop that caters to a design-savvy crowd.)

Check off the following relevant pros and cons to make the decision that's best for you.

Pros

_____ Cold cash. There's no shame in doing what it takes to bring in an income.

_____ Confidence. Sometimes you need a legitimate reason to get up and get dressed (in something other than sweats) each day. Having a place to report for work and connecting with people who'll rely on your performance is a confidence booster.

_____ Current experience. Closing the gap in unemployment can make your résumé more marketable, especially if you're able to spin the job into something positive.

_____ Contacts. You're not going to find work sitting at home. Even if it's a retail job, that customer you serve or that co-worker in the break room may just be the ones who offer a new lead or two.

Cons

_____ Low pay. Sure it's better to bring in something than nothing, but don't expect big bucks in a short-term survival job.

_____ Lots of jobs. Great employers don't like to see too many positions, especially short-lived posts, on a résumé. You'll wind up working overtime to finesse the experience into a good thing.

_____ Limited job-search time. If you're working while looking for the ideal job, your search time is far more limited. That will require you to be extremely disciplined to juggle both.

_____ Little (if any) growth. Survival posts are often hourly, temporary positions without near-term advancement opportunity. But everything has its purpose.

If you opt to go for it, remember that it's nobody's business that you earned more at your previous job. Knock that I'm-better-than-this chip off your shoulder and proudly perform your job. Be grateful that you beat out what was presumably stiff competition for the role. And keep searching for the job you really want.

THE FOUR Cs

What employers are looking for—on your résumé, in your interview, and when you get that job—are the Four Cs.

Credentials: Do you have the specific skills and knowledge gained through education and/or experience to do the job?

Competence: Are you any good at those skills?

Character: What kind of person are you and will you be a good fit for the culture?

Commitment: Are you ready to get your hands dirty and prove to be a success in this role?

Using all that you've learned so far, now it's your job to show off your Four Cs, using them to their best advantage.

When you search for job leads or go out to an interview, listen to Queen's "We Will Rock You" or Kelly Clarkson's "Breakaway" (or another song that always puts you in a good mood) and think about your Four Cs, the reasons why you deserve that job.

CHAPTER 5

Ain't No Mountain High Enough

Overcoming setbacks and obstacles

After the 9/11 terrorist attacks, we had our biggest Women For Hire career fair ever in New York. The turnout even surprised those of us who were planning it, in no small part because it took place just a month after that terrible day. New York City was still reeling from the blow of the attacks, and another punch was coming—an economic free fall. That meant layoffs and hiring freezes. We thought we'd have to cancel the event.

But surprises were in store. All the registered companies we called said they'd be there and not just to show solidarity for the city: They had vacant positions they needed to fill.

And so we got a lot of media attention. One reporter dubbed it, "the event of hiring and hope." There was great buzz and a really good feeling throughout the city about our expo; it was a sign that New York may be down, but not out. We were thrilled to be part of it.

The day before the event was to start, I got a phone call from former President Clinton. I was certain that the call was actually from my husband who decided to play a joke on me—something he's perfectly able and inclined to do with a little voice disguise. Thank goodness I didn't mouth off, because the real Bill Clinton was indeed on the line. He said that at the core of our financial freedom and independence is our right to work. He encouraged me to keep up all my efforts.

That 30-second conversation inspires me to this day. It's been a number of years since that call, and when I share that anecdote I get two very distinct responses.

Reaction one: "You go, girl! Regardless of your political preference, getting recognized for your work by a former U.S. president is a pretty cool thing." I happen to agree with that.

Reaction two (usually conveyed in a look but not always): "My, aren't you quite pleased with yourself, to tell us you got a call from Clinton." Ouch.

The reality is that both have the ring of truth. I was thrilled to be recognized for my work, and I was pretty darn pleased with myself. And I had every right to be. Pride in my company and the work we do is what enables us to get up every morning and do what we do with gusto and passion. And recognition for our efforts is the cherry on the sundae.

Blah: "It was no big deal."

Ah!: "Yes, I'm very proud of getting that recognition."

Every person should celebrate his or her victories. We all have those moments of which we're particularly proud, but I've noticed that too many women celebrate in silence. We shy away from taking the credit we deserve for fear of being thought of as conceited or arrogant. That little voice, first heard in the halls of elementary school and now in our heads, tells us not to be a show-off, and we wind up running away from our accomplishments rather than celebrating them. Fear of self-promotion is the sticky floor that keeps so many of us standing still.

And then—even worse than that nagging fear—there's self-doubt.

Have you ever applied to a job, sat through an interview only to think along the following lines:

"I'm old enough to be the boss's mother."

"I've been out of the loop, raising my kids for fifteen years."

"There's just no work in my area."

"They told me my credit wasn't good enough to get a job."

"Nobody wants a new grad with no experience."

I regularly get e-mails and calls from people expressing feelings like these. With this mind-set, you're firing yourself before you even apply for a job. This same defeatist attitude stops many employed women for asking for a promotion or the money they deserve.

Is it fear of rejection? Fear of humiliation? Or just plain fear of that two letter word *no*?

You must get over it. Don't let that fear of rejection keep you from asking for what you deserve or keep you from putting yourself out there. Women have to take a cue from guys and toughen enough a bit to speak up for what we want and deserve. Stop holding yourself back! Now's the time to turn that thinking around:

"Older workers are employed in every organization."

"I'm getting into the swing of things, and I'm ready to recommit myself to my career."

"Surely somebody's hiring here, and I'm determined to find that person."

"I can confidently explain my financial situation, including the steps I'm taking to improve it."

"New grads are hired into entry level roles every single day."

Force yourself to see the glass as half full, not half empty. If you think your chances are only one in a thousand, what are you going to do to make sure you're that one?

Consider that each time you hear a no, it means you're one step closer to finding the yes. Because every no you hear is the result of the fact that:

- You actually made a cold call.

- You went on an interview.

- You applied for a job online.

- You showed up.

- You took a chance by putting yourself out there.

In other words, you tried. And with every no, you've learned something, a clue about why you're hearing those no's. If you're receiving rejections, ask for feedback. Ask the person to be candid in sharing with you why you're not being considered and what you could do differently to improve your chances. For example, you may say, "While I enjoyed our conversations and I wish I was the successful candidate for this position, I'm hoping you would con- sider providing me with some candid feedback on what I might do differently next time and what it was about the applicant you selected, especially because I'm extremely committed to this line of work." Maybe you can turn those no's into the information you need to get that yes.

A woman I know who worked in recruitment for a medical device manufacturer applied for a position as a recruiter in finance. The person responsible for filling the position thanked her for applying but said he didn't think she was the right fit for the role. Instead of simply deleting his e-mail, she wrote back asking for his feedback on why he felt that way. He said he really wanted someone with experience recruiting finance candidates. My friend explained that when she joined the medical device manufacturer, she didn't have that industry knowledge, but she was able to learn it very quickly. What she did have—and what she could bring to this financial giant— were the core competencies to be a very successful recruiter, which would translate to other fields. He agreed and invited her to interview. By probing, she turned the no to a maybe—and ultimately she turned it into a yes and got the job. Take note: you should ask for feedback when you've been turned away.

I equate this to our personal lives as well. Many of my single girlfriends often ask me, "When am I going to get married?" My answer is always, "Uh, when you start dating. Unless you put yourself out there, you have no chance of finding the right person." Similarly, guys are often comfortable jumping into a game of pick-up basketball with total strangers. That's a tactic that you must apply off the court as well. You have no chance of getting the job of your dreams if you don't try.

Really Ready to Change

Anyone who is having difficulty overcoming challenges and navigating this job market must also be ready to embrace change, which is easier said than done. My favorite book on the issue of change is *Who Moved My Cheese?* (Pick up a copy or borrow one—with 24 million in print, someone you know is bound to have it.) Dr. Spencer Johnson tells a super simple tale about a very complex issue. This quick read—in under an hour you'll go from cover to cover—makes clear the dangers of sticking with the status quo. The four characters have grown accustomed to finding their cheese in the same spot every day—day after day. Even as the supply dwindles, it doesn't occur to them that someday soon it may be gone. When it finally disappears, some characters instantly recognize the need to scramble and scurry to find another source of cheese, while another resists change. Instead, that character gets angry and frustrated about this sudden change and is totally unwilling to adapt to the new reality. Read in amazement what happens when someone absolutely refuses to try something new or move in a different direction.

The message is clear for all of us: Even if you've always done one thing one way, there's a very good chance it won't always be viable. You'll have to change or you'll risk extinction, which is an unacceptable alternative. This is true with job titles, career choices, and search strategies. When something isn't working, be open to exploration and change. If not, you'll find that it's impossible to meet your goals.

Face the Music

There are several common obstacles people face when looking for work, some of which relate to numbers: age, years out of the job market, the strength of the local economy, and a credit score. Let's take them on one by one.

Does Age Matter?

Before blind musical auditions—where the performer is heard, but not seen—became common in the seventies, just 10 percent of new hires at major U.S. orchestras were women. The theory was that women weren't very good musicians and couldn't hold their own against male counterparts. Labor unions began protesting the hiring process and pushing for blind auditions where musicians would try out behind a curtain so appearance, gender, and age were concealed.

In a study published in a 2000 issue of the *American Economic Review*, a review of personnel from eleven major orchestras by Harvard economist Claudia Goldin and Princeton's Cecelia Rouse found that 29 percent of females and 20 percent of males advanced to the final round in blind auditions. When auditions were not blind, only 19 percent of women advanced compared to 23 percent of men. Even though sex discrimination is hard to measure, those statistics speak volumes. Fortunately, since the eighties, about half the news hires at the New York Philharmonic, 40 percent at the San Francisco Symphony, and more than a third in Boston and Chicago have been women.

That report always has me wondering what the workplace would look like right now if all interviews were conducted blind, where recruiters and hiring managers had no idea of your gender, age, or looks. (A girl's allowed to dream, right?)

To those who say age is just a number, I say, yeah, and denial is a river in Egypt. (Bada boom!) There are real prejudices against older workers—and sometimes younger ones too. I hear from women in their twenties and thirties who tell me they fear they're being rejected because they look too young to step into a specific role. On the flip side employers call Women For Hire looking to fill a particularly challenging or important position all the time, and they often start the conversation with, "I am looking for a young hot shot." And almost always our response is, "Would you consider an old hot shot?"

And they chuckle nervously thinking, yeah, I guess I really shouldn't say that. But my position is, they shouldn't *think* that either.

On the issue of age and generational diversity, it's not enough what we say but it's also really important how we think. The see-saw economy means that workers who thought they were going to retire will have to stay on the job. Even so, Generation Y—those individuals born between 1977 and 2000—now make up the largest segment of the population at nearly 80 million strong.

That means that more generations will be working side by side than ever before. It is inevitable that you will be working with or for people who are from a different generation than you are. No longer is hierarchy or success determined by age or longevity. If you're going to be part of the new job market, you'll have to accept this simple truth.

But you can rise above the barriers and get the job you want. Here's how to do it.

ARE YOU UP FOR IT?

Could you take orders from an employer your child's age? Could you work with your granddaughter? Not everyone can do it. Many older workers believe that their young colleagues are inexperienced, impatient, and immature. If you are going to work in today's workplace, rid yourself of that prejudice before you even apply. Remember that you were in their shoes when you began your career, and you'll find them much easier to understand. If you honestly think you can't do it, don't waste your time or the employer's time and money training you. There are other work opportunities, such as starting your own business, that may be a better fit. So really think this through before moving on to the next step.

SET THE RECORD STRAIGHT

I've noticed how people often say, "You'd be bored," when what they really want to say is, "You're too old." With the exception of some government positions with age limits for applicants, nobody can legally come out and say that age is a factor. If you ever suspect that age might be an issue and hear those words, instead of appearing like a deer in the headlights, be prepared with an answer. Your response should acknowledge the issue and turn it into a positive.

For example: "I appreciate what you're saying, and I've got to tell you one of the benefits of having experience is the wisdom and perspective of knowing not to put myself in a position in which I'd be bored because that would be the kiss of death for both of us. I certainly wouldn't want to be unchallenged, but I thought a lot about this opportunity before I applied for it and I wish that we could continue this dialogue before you simply rule me out based on an assumption that I'm not the right fit. The experience that I bring, perhaps more than what the typical candidate has, could actually work to your advantage and mine."

An answer like that accomplishes a number of things. It tells the interviewer that you understand his or her concern and have considered it before you applied. You're also offering a bonus—priceless experience the company can rely on when the going gets tough.

Blah: "Yeah, I guess I'm not right because you really need someone who has done this before."

Ah!: "I bring a great deal of experience to the position. I'm a quick study, and I'm eager to learn from my new colleagues, too."

KEEP YOUR RÉSUMÉ CURRENT

Your résumé is your calling card so it must be up to date. Tailor it to the position you're applying for and be selective about what you include. Think relevant experience and skills only. You don't have to include the year you got your degree because the number could startle the interviewer and may undermine your confidence.

Your résumé must also be up to date in the language you use to describe your experience. You must use current industry terms. I received a résumé from a woman who listed a position in which she used a ditto machine. Most interviewers today have never heard of a ditto machine. I've also seen résumés without e-mail addresses. E-mail is the prevalent form of business communication today; there's just no such thing as being a technophobe in the current marketplace. If you want a job in today's workplace, your résumé has to convey that you know what goes on there.

If you haven't worked much in the last year, use only the year on your résumé, not the month and the year. For example, if you held just one short-term position in 2008, instead of indicating June 2008 to August 2008, simply list 2008 only. Leave it to the interviewer to ask for details.

Don't include 30 years of work history. Limit your résumé to the last 10 to 15 years of work experience. That's all you're really judged on these days. Remove the date(s) of college graduation.

KEEP YOURSELF CURRENT

Another concern employers have about older workers is that they may not be up on the latest technology and, worse, may be reluctant to use it. Expect to be asked about your skill level. You also need to be able to speak the language of your co-workers. That doesn't mean you have to keep up on what's happening on *The Hills*. Younger workers have grown up communicating via text messages, instant messaging, and e-mail, and so they bring those methods to work. You have to be able to do the same, even if you prefer face-to-face communication. Don't mistake Twitter, a popular micro-blogging site, for a twit.

If you're not as savvy about technology as you should be, get up to speed with a course at a local learning center or college or ask a friend (or that friend's kid or grandkid) to help you out. I've seen many people lose out on temp jobs because they can't pass the proficiency tests in Microsoft Word or PowerPoint. If this is happening to you, don't ignore it. Take a short course. Most companies have their own specialized software that all employees have to learn, but you'll feel more confident and you'll be more qualified if you bring the basic skills to the table and that could be the difference between getting hired or not.

"Current" can also be defined by education. If you know your skills and knowledge are outdated or if you don't have the necessary training for your field of choice, then some training is essential. First, check with your state's department of labor to determine if you qualify for free or reduced-cost training through funds provided by the federal stimulus package. (Before you assume there's nothing for you, consider the money you'd save if you at least invest the time to research the possibilities.) With so many online courses and local colleges offering full- and part-time programs, there is truly something for every budget, all areas of study, and multiple skill levels.

KEEP IT TO YOURSELF

Younger workers live different lives than you did at their age. Their values, work ethics, and expectations will not match yours. Unless it directly affects your work, keep your opinions on their behavior and lifestyle to yourself. Instead of pointing out the errors of their ways, just be glad you're not their mom or dad.

Blah: "I did this job before anyone needed a computer."

Ah!: "I'm taking a class to keep up on the latest technology because that's how the world operates today."

LEARN FROM THE YOUNG'UNS

You may have entered the workforce when time served drove raises and promotions. It doesn't work that way anymore. Twentysomethings change jobs every 18 months, and the average American will have held 10 positions between the ages of 18 and 38, according to the Bureau of Labor Statistics. Because they are used to these short stints, they believe performance and results should drive compensation and promotion. They're more apt to ask for a raise after doing a great job on a big project after only six months. They have no qualms about asking to leapfrog titles and positions without regard to protocol that was historically based on age.

The same is true if you work for a younger person. The boss's perspective—not yours—will likely determine raises and promotions. In an interview, you should ask the boss outright what his or her philosophy is on awarding raises and promotions. "What must I do to earn more money or be promoted?" Asking directly helps avoid any misunderstandings, and lets the boss know that you are eager to get to work hard and succeed.

Victim Language

"It's so easy to feel like a victim. Feeling guilty is a waste of time," says *Good Morning America*'s financial contributor Mellody Hobson. "You choose your life, and if you don't like something, you can choose to change it."

At her Chicago financial services firm, Ariel Investments, Mellody says colleagues call each other out when they hear "victim language."

Example?

I'll say, "Wow, that client was just so mean to me," and my colleagues will say, "victim language" because that's how I chose to interpret the conversation. I didn't have to interpret it that way. We don't accept it when an employee blames someone else for something not getting done. That's 'victim language.'"

PEERAGE

There are jobs and online job boards geared to older workers. Among the top fields tapping these mature workers: healthcare, education, retail, financial services, temporary services, and even engineering and sciences. The trucking industry is looking for older workers on the theory that if they can drive a Winnebago into the sunset, they can handle an 18-wheeler, too.

The websites of organizations like Experience Works, Workforce50, Senior Job Bank, Seniors4Hire, and YourEncore specialize in supporting workers from fiftysomethings to retirees. In addition, AARP's National Employer Team and RetirementJobs have jobs for national employers that are eager to tap into the 50+ market.

Mom's Second Act

Alexandra Pelosi has made a name for herself with her quirky documentaries, starting with *Journeys with George*, the film she made with her handheld camera about George Bush when she covered his 2000 campaign for NBC News.

She is also the daughter of House Speaker Nancy Pelosi, who she says could be a poster child for second acts in life.

Nancy Pelosi raised five children before first running for Congress in 1987, when her last child, Alexandra, had gone off to college.

"She drove carpools. She made our Halloween costumes by hand. She planned our birthday parties. She was a mom," Alexandra told WomenForHire.com. "It was the empty nest syndrome that brought her to Congress. She did this as an afterthought. After five kids, you have a lot of energy, and you don't sleep at night so she had a lot of free time on her hands. So she went to Congress.

"My mom was always on the cutting edge," Alexandra says. "She likes to tell her friends that I said to her when she went to Congress, 'Mom, you're a pioneer.' And she said, 'Why, because I'm a woman in Congress?' And I said, 'No, because you stopped cooking before all the other moms did.'"

Years out of the Workplace

Women who have been out of the workforce caring for their families will encounter many of the same attitudes faced by older workers, plus another one that is just as tough: the résumé gap.

Meryl Streep took a few years off in the middle of her career to spend more time with her four children. She lost key years at a crucial time in her career—her late forties—not knowing if she would find meaningful roles when she was ready to come back. Of course, having a few Academy Awards in her pocket didn't hurt when she was ready to return to work. If you aren't packing Oscars, you have to do some groundwork.

ARE YOU REALLY READY TO RETURN?

Ask yourself this question before an interviewer does. If you want to get back to work but have time restrictions—as in "I can work only four hours on Monday and I need Friday afternoons off"—you're actually feeding into the concerns the interviewer already has. Instead, think long-term. Don't hold out for the dream corporate job: focus on part-time or freelance jobs that fit in with your current time commitment. You can start filling in the time gap and maybe work your way up to the position you really want.

MAKE NO APOLOGIES

Be proud of your choice to focus on your family. Instead of trying to hide those years out of the workforce, turn time out into time well spent. Take what you've been doing and spin it into skills that are relevant to what you want to do next. If you've renovated your home, explain that enormous undertaking. If you've been caring for elderly parents, talk about how you've managed their care. If you've navigated the college admissions process for your kids, discuss that process.

Don't forget your volunteerism. Long-term commitments matter most, not writing a check or spending a day at the recycling center. You want to show that you're focused and can follow through on a project over the long haul. Be able explain a meaningful contribution with a positive outcome.

Turn that time spent juggling carpools and play dates and volunteering at the local library into strengths. "While I was raising my children, I learned that one of my great talents is my ability to prioritize. Managing the schedule of a busy family and focusing on the daily details of children and a husband has actually improved my skills to handle many projects at once. Plus, I'm definitely an exceptional negotiator. If we're making a family decision and one kid feels left out or is unhappy, nobody wins. My role is ensuring that everyone is satisfied with an outcome."

The idea is to turn these life experiences into a showcase of your skills and success. You don't have to explain what you did quite literally every single day; instead, focus on these big picture examples. Mention that you cared for an elderly or sick relative, managed the college admissions process for your kids, oversaw a home renovation, planned a cross-country move, trailed a spouse's career, and anything else that's relevant.

Your attitude toward your time off will directly influence the interviewer's—make sure you are confident that you're ready to get the job. Practice the way you talk about your experiences with a friend or family member. You want to present a confident, assured face to an interviewer.

LOOK THE PART

I got lots of nasty e-mails after a local TV segment in Atlanta when a caller asked if I thought it was necessary for graying women to color their hair to get hired. I said I wouldn't use the word *necessary*, but I couldn't sugarcoat my response either: Yes, in some cases it's harder for a woman with gray hair to get hired than it is for her brunette counterpart. (The same isn't always true for men, though we'll see how the recession and the tarnished image of Wall Street executives impacts that.) Several women were furious that I didn't chastise employers for age bias.

My work is about helping someone get hired right now. We can call some employers on the carpet for their recruitment practices, but it takes time to turn the tide. That doesn't help the woman who needs a job today. So while we should all fight the good fight for the long haul to help future generations of men and women face more equality and less bias in the workplace, we must also adjust to the realities of our current climate.

Go with the hair color that makes you feel your best. A ditzy blonde wouldn't be my pick over the graying granny. Accessories, such as hip glasses or modern shoes, can take ten years off anyone, which can make a twentysomething appear too youthful or can allow a fiftysomething to leave them guessing.

Teeth whitening gained in popularity among jobseekers who recognized that smoke and coffee-stained teeth don't do much for their image. Fortunately there are inexpensive options on the market so the benefits are accessible to anyone.

Go with Your Gut

New York anchorwoman Lori Stokes says that life should never be easy.

"A couple of knocks along the way give you character and toughen you up. I've faced both racism and sexism in the workplace, at the hands of presidents, general managers, news directors, and even co-anchors."

That's not all. "I've been told everything from 'You should stick with your own kind' when I was dating my soon-to-be Caucasian husband to 'You certainly don't need breast implants' when I was pregnant and discussing an upcoming series on breast implants with a boss."

Lori says that an incident in 1991, when she was a reporter at a Fox station in Baltimore, has guided her ever since.

For the first time her father—former U.S. Representative Carl Stokes—faced a tough reelection back home in Ohio. Sensing he needed her help, she went to her news director to ask that she be allowed to go home and campaign for him. Answer: no. She appealed to the general manager and to the owners of her TV station. Request denied.

But Lori felt compelled to go, and so she flew back home to Cleveland. When she returned the next day, on her desk was a letter saying she had been fired. "I had one hour to clean out my desk and leave the premises, with an escort."

Two weeks later, a news director at the ABC affiliate in Washington D.C., called her. "He liked that I put family first and told me to come in for an interview. He hired me the next day. Six months later I became the 6 and 11 P.M. news anchor."

Lori is now the anchor of the top-rated local morning news on WABC in New York. "My philosophy reads like a string of clichés, but it's what I live by. Go with your gut, be true to yourself, never let them see you sweat, and no regrets. There is always something better around the bend."

BE READY TO GO

Be ready to assure an interviewer that your responsibilities at home—child or eldercare—are covered. Don't fake it. Instead, have everything in place before you embark on your search and certainly before sitting down for an interview. Depending on the conversation, if you sense some concern on the part of a contact or perspective employer, be proactive. For example, you might say, "After spending three years devoted exclusively to my family, I'm thrilled that my kids are more self-sufficient and I have wonderful, reliable childcare in place. Now I'm confident in focusing on my career because professional growth is a priority." Granted, an employer shouldn't ask about your family status or childcare needs, so they're not entitled to this information. But if you present it in the right way, it'll help erase concerns that your intuition tells you exists.

Bottom line: You have to make it as easy as possible for an employer to hire you. Don't let him or her think you'll have a learning curve that's steeper than figuring out the location of the restroom or a period of adjustment that will last longer than a week.

GET OFF THE NET

If you are looking for a job and presently have a gap in your résumé, get off the Internet and get out of the house. Scouring job boards and posting your résumé online is not enough at this point. Recruiters I speak to admit that when looking at two résumés— one with current experience, one with a gap—they always go for the current one. This means you have to do everything possible to bypass the online application process and go straight to the decision makers. You must be in the room with the recruiter to turn that missing time into something interesting and positive. It's your personality and passion that can help overcome the gap, and that can be accomplished only in person. I'm sure you could sell yourself if only you were given the chance.

GET IN THE DOOR

Start by meeting people the same way you do in other aspects of life: through mutual friends and contacts. Connect with the people closest to you first. My kids routinely tell classmates whose parents are out of work to have those moms or dads call me. Reconnect with former colleagues and working friends. If your networking turns up contacts but not necessarily open positions, you should still pursue face-to-face informational meetings. Offer to take the new contact out for coffee or to meet them at his or her office for 15 to 20 minutes. When you sit down with these busy people, be very clear about your goals and what you hope they can do to help you. Convince them that you *are* returning to your career, not just that you hope to, so sitting down with you will not be a waste of time. And remember the Rule of Three: You should try to get three new contacts from every meeting, cup of coffee, or phone call. It's the way to rebuild your professional database. And then be sure to follow up on those leads in a timely manner.

Another great way to reiterate your commitment to getting back to work is by joining a professional group in your industry. You'll find associations in every field and your current affiliations should be included on your résumé.

PLAY THE FIELD

Don't limit your job search to the types of positions you had before your time out. You left the workplace to reinvent yourself as a homemaker. Now it's time to reinvent yourself again. Separate your actual skills from the sign on your old office door. A medical billing clerk can put her financial know-how to use in an electronics company or a retail store. A hospitality sales executive can switch from that hard-hit industry to a medical services sales role, which is going strong.

Example: I know a woman who worked for several years as a chef before she got pregnant, but the late-night hours weren't conducive to raising children. Five years later, when she was ready to go back to work, she got a job at a popular community center teaching cooking classes. She took her cooking skills and what she learned at home about teaching her children and turned them into a new career—one in which she does what she loves in a setting that works for her family.

Blah to *Ah!*: Looking Professional

When you walk into an office or a coffee shop for a meeting of any kind—a formal interview or an informational meeting—you have to look like a professional, not a mom fitting the meeting in between soccer practice and ballet lessons. Stay-at-home moms should dress the part and wear makeup to distance themselves from the playground look. Even a bit of makeup conveys that you are a polished professional at a time when you need it most. Out of practice? Stop into a Sephora for a free makeup application a few hours before the interview.

When No One's Hiring

Another obstacle many people face is geographical. There are cities, like Detroit, that are truly company towns. If you find yourself looking for a job in a city that's struggling, you may have to cast your net virtually to get hired.

I have hammered home (and will continue to do so) the importance of face-to-face contact with employers. But this is a new world, one in which some employers have found it more cost effective to export jobs half a world away than provide an office for employees to work in. There's no reason those same employers can't export that same job to your home office.

We maintain friendships despite great distances and have clients and colleagues in branch offices we've never met. There's no reason why you can't get customers and clients who'll hire you long distance as well. This kind of networking is all on the phone, via e-mail, and even via Skype and video chat. It can be done, but it takes initiative.

YOU'RE MORE THAN YOUR RÉSUMÉ

You are more than the positions you have held. It's time to adapt to the marketplace. Just because you've always worked as an auditor at an automaker doesn't mean you can't take your skills in a new direction.

Example: A woman I worked with in Michigan needed to rebuild a once-lucrative photography career launched largely through assignments from the automotive industry, which have now all but disappeared. I helped her see that she could apply her creative skills far beyond cars. We broadened her client base online and she landed projects shooting photos for skin-care products, a corporate brochure, and even artwork for customized Mother's Day cards. Instead of focusing only on the automotive industry, she could photograph corporate events, family portraits, and weddings. Her project budgets must also change—from big-budget shoots to small projects as low as just a couple hundred dollars now that the marketplace has slowed considerably.

This flexibility can work in almost all fields. If you were an investment analyst on Wall Street, you could leverage your skills to start a business, join a consulting firm, or teach at a business school. An out-of-work newspaper reporter can move into public relations, speechwriting for corporate executives, and writing for anything from textbooks to websites.

A rug salesperson may decide to pursue a sales role in a totally different industry, in which case all of her communication should focus on sales: her volume of monthly or quarterly sales, the number of accounts she opens or maintains, a record of exceeding sales quotas and more. This emphasizes her ability to sell, not merely her connection to rugs. On the flip side, she might want to move from a career in rug sales to become a textile designer. In such a case, she'll highlight her depth of knowledge of rug colors, patterns, weaves, and history, as well as her eye for décor and design. She'll lessen the hype of her sales skill and hype her passion for the product and its range.

This model applies to many areas of expertise. You don't have to do what you've always done—but you have to know where your skills can be leveraged.

CAN YOU WORK FROM HOME?

Are you a self-starter? Someone who can focus on a task without the boss breathing down your neck? If the answer is no, there's nothing to be ashamed of. Many of us thrive when working collaboratively, and many of us are easily distracted when there's a fridge, phone, and TV nearby just waiting for us to pay them a visit. If you need outside stimulation to get your work mojo on, online or phone work may not be for you. However, if you work well on your own, working online from home may be the answer to your prayers.

VIRTUALLY THERE

There are now dozens of job titles that begin with the word *virtual*. All of us interact with these workers more often than we may imagine. Customer service representatives, technical support, travel agents, and fund-raisers—those voices on the phone may be working wearing slippers, while their kids are napping in the next room.

Think about it. Does a bookkeeper and billing assistant need to be in the office? If her work is computerized and the office computers are networked, there is no reason she needs to be in the office— or the same city—as her employer to do her work. I'll give you the specifics on how to work from home in Chapter 7.

GET-THE-JOB TRAINING

If your skills need updating, unemployment offers an opportunity to learn new skills or improve existing ones through online and classroom learning. There are a number of free and low-cost resources available nationwide serving individuals at all skill levels.

Government Programs

Government programs, such as Career One Stop and Career Voyages, offer training as well as job placement assistance. Career

Voyages also provides access to apprenticeship and certificate programs in the areas that the Bureau of Labor Statistics determines are high-growth positions for both blue- and white-collar workers.

Nonprofits

Nonprofit organizations also offer training and placement assistance. For example, Jewish Vocational Service (JVS), a non-sectarian agency founded during the Great Depression to assist immigrants with job training and placement, now operates 22 agencies throughout the country, serving nearly a half million people with a wide range of career-related services. More than 25,000 individuals were placed in jobs last year as a result of the training they received. And JVS works with 40,000 employers of all sizes. The organization gets to know the business needs in its area and can customize training programs to meet the demands in a variety of industries.

Similar skills training and placement services are offered through Goodwill, which says it places someone in a good job every 53 seconds of every business day. There are 161 Goodwill community-based locations in the United States that offer job training programs in a variety of industries, including healthcare, hospitality, banking, information technology, and computer programming. Neither of these groups are limited to blue-collar jobs by any means.

Temp Agencies

Many temp agencies offer free tutorials designed to help improve the skill level of their candidates. For example, a retired accountant who is looking to get back to work can sign up with Robert Half, which specializes in placing accounting and finance professionals and has access to 8,000 online tutorials that cover everything from technical accounting skills to leadership and public speaking.

Back to School?

When they can't get a job, some people go back to school, assuming this is the ticket to employment. Sometimes it is, but don't assume that without another degree it's impossible to land a job, or that with more degrees more jobs will suddenly materialize. Try telling that to PhDs who are now dumbing down their resumes because they have been constantly labeled "overqualified."

Yes, on average the higher the degree the greater your earning power. But a prestigious MBA program can easily cost $50,000, plus living expenses. Add that to the balance on your current student loan and what do you get? Enormous debt before you earn a penny.

So don't go back to school full-time simply because you can't find a job. Exhaust your job search options before committing to a costly program and even then, research the availability of funds to cover your education. For example, consider taking a lesser position with a company that provides tuition reimbursement, so you learn on its time and dime. Check with your state's unemployment office to find free or low-cost training programs you may qualify for. Look into scholarships through local schools.

Bottom line: education should benefit your long-term career goals and not simply be a crutch in a tough job market.

Community Colleges and Online Universities

There are more than 1,000 community colleges in the United States that offer degrees and certifications. If you're considering such a school or an online university, ask about financial aid and job placement assistance. Find out about employers who hire from the program, ask about the employment rate of its most recent class of graduates, and consider that when deciding on a program for you.

One caveat: Historically, when unemployment rises so do college enrollments. And although it may seem that being out of work would be a good time to pursue your education, don't assume that another certificate or degree will automatically generate job offers. You can look at the Bureau of Labor Statistics website (bls.gov) for information for demand for a specific degree.

Returnships

A groundbreaking program at Sara Lee offers paid, four- to six-month internships to people who have been out of the job market for three to five years. The "returnships" are available at the Sara Lee headquarters in marketing, accounting, sales, finance, and the legal department. The program was launched by company CEO Brenda Barnes, who left PepsiCo in 1997 to raise her children. Now she's back in the corner office, reaching out to others who are trying to get back in the game.

Externships

Think of an externship as an internship for people who are no longer students. Even though it will likely be unpaid (or you may negotiate a small stipend) this is a chance to gain current experience, which ultimately can be leveraged for a new paid position. Benefits of an externship include:

- Exposure to another profession along with first-hand access to the realities (highs and lows) of a variety of specific positions.

- The ability to develop new skills and build your existing skills by contributing to daily tasks and special projects.

- Current experience to include on your resume, which can be leveraged when applying for your next paid position.

- Access to new contacts to form and nurture professional relationships in your field.

- Long-term value derived from a short-term time commitment.

These benefits are especially valuable to someone who is focused on closing a gap in work history, gaining new skills, or switching fields entirely. Externships may range from three to six months, during which time you can work in one department or propose a rotation. (While you can certainly propose less than three months, many employers will frown on the idea of investing in getting to know you, training you, and involving you in projects if you're only there for a few weeks.)

When I google the phrase *externship resources,* I get more than 100,000 hits, some of which are connected to university programs. Do your own search and visit the sites that pop up to find companies and government agencies with programs already in place. In absence of a formal program, you can pitch yourself as an extern, which is likely to have a better reception among small- and medium-size employers. There is less bureaucracy in a smaller shop than in a giant corporation, which is a good thing since you're probably looking for a quick turnaround on this proposal.

Just as you're applying to several jobs at any one time, you should pitch an externship to multiple employers at once as well. Use your networks to find prospective employers, and cold call or contact the employers on your wish list. Since you don't know who'll accept your proposal, you must have lots of feelers out there.

Then follow up. While it'd be easy to assume that your brilliant proposal will result in instant phone calls asking when you can start, the reality is it'll likely take extensive follow-up on your part to get in the door. That's to be expected, so don't be discouraged by the process.

A general template for an externship proposal can be found in the box below. Customize it as necessary:

Externship Proposal Template

Date: [Today's date]
To: [Prospective employer]
From: [You]

I respectfully request your consideration to create an externship opportunity for me to contribute to the *[department]* at *[employer]*. This would create a win–win for both of us: You'd benefit from three months *[specify your desired length of service]* of my service at no cost and no obligation to you, and in return I'd gain valuable hands-on experience, which would aid my professional development.

Please think of an externship similar to a traditional internship, except instead of accepting a college student, you'd be agreeing to take on a professional who is out of school and can focus total attention on the position for career advancement purposes.

In addition to a great degree of enthusiasm and a commitment to excellence, I'd bring you *[name the specific knowledge, skills, and abilities you possess]*, which I am confident would benefit your organization.

Because I know this is a relatively new concept and not something that's in practice now at your organization, I've taken the liberty to propose the suggested terms and conditions of such an opportunity for your review. This is just a starting point and I'm open to discussing changes in these terms to serve both of our needs and interests.

Duration of externship: *[Start date]* to *[End date]*

Anticipated hours per week: *[Number and times]*

Desired department(s) for assignment: *[Where you want to work and why]*

I agree that during this time I will not be an employee of *[company]*, and my externship activities are subject to termination at any time for any reason. Further, I also agree that I am not entitled to compensation during the externship, nor am I entitled to a job at the conclusion of the externship. *[If you'd like to propose a stipend to cover travel and lunch expenses, for example, this is the place to do it.]* The purpose of this externship training is equivalent to the work experience for a vocational school or professional degree program and is merely an adjunct to such studies. *[The purpose of this statement is to make it clear that you're not technically working for free, which can be challenged by law. Instead, you're receiving valuable training and experience in lieu of a salary. This minimizes an employer's liability for allowing you to serve as an extern.]*

You have nothing to lose, and we both have so much to gain if you'd entertain this three-month proposal. I'd bring you my skills and determination and I know I'd walk away with great insights and experience from my time with your organization. I'd be happy to discuss this in depth at your convenience. Thank you very much for your time and consideration.

Work for Free? Keep an Open Mind

Jessica Guff spent 25 years as a top producer at ABC News in New York.

But early on in her career, after graduating from Harvard in 1982 with a master's degree in history, nobody was knocking on her door to hire her.

To get her foot in television, Jessica volunteered to help a producer/correspondent at ABC News by doing research on her own time and dime. Her mom supported her while she worked day and night for three months.

"I'm a big believer in doing whatever it takes—even working for free—for the right job," Jessica says.

It paid off.

"Once a freelance position opened up, I got retroactive back pay and the opportunity to work at ABC News for the next quarter century," she says. "Once you get your foot in the door you have a chance to show them that you have what it takes to stay and move up. Go for it, even if it means living with your parents and forgoing nights out on the town."

Background Checks

You may be reading this book because you're returning to work out of financial necessity. In the current economy, you may be dealing with a foreclosure or other financial defaults. No matter what the cause, you're seriously struggling to make ends meet.

Some 80 percent of Americans, according to a Visa survey, don't realize that credit history can be used in preemployment screening. Many employers use credit history as a measure of judgment and character. If you can't manage your financial obligations, they wonder if it's a sign of irresponsibility or untrustworthiness.

Critics of this practice say it's unfair for personal credit history to be used when judging professional qualifications. They say there's no link between poor credit and job performance. Many of these people have hit rough patches, especially during a recession, and now they're caught in a vicious circle: To pay down their debt, they need a job, but they can't get hired because of their debt. (Incidentally, several states are pursuing legislation that would block employers from using credit checks during the employment screening process.)

Fair or not, think of it from the employer's point of view. They are searching for someone who they can trust with the keys to the front door, the money in the till, and trade secrets that make their business a success. Would you choose the applicant with a good credit history, or one who has struggled to pay his own bills?

For any job that gives you access to valuables—money, products, technology, trade secrets, you should expect a credit check. But it's by no means limited solely to those areas; employers use their own discretion when deciding which positions to screen.

Bad credit, now what? If you have poor credit, it doesn't automatically mean you're unemployable. You should focus on these steps so you don't lose out on positions.

GET THE FACTS

Check your credit report, whether you're applying for a job or not. Under federal law, you have the right to receive a free copy of your credit report once every 12 months from each of the three nationwide consumer-reporting companies. (Visit annualcreditreport.com, which is the only truly free service to access those reports.) Immediately address any mistakes you find on the report with the creditor.

DON'T BE SURPRISED

Under federal law, you have to give permission for employers to conduct background checks, including credit checks, so none of this happens behind your back.

Whenever you sign an employment application, read the fine print. Most of the time, you're signing a consent and disclosure clause that grants your permission to the employer and its designated third party vendor(s) to conduct a background check. Be aware of what exactly you're agreeing to upfront.

WATCH FOR SKELETONS IN THE CLOSET

The majority of employers today use some form of background check as part of their due diligence. By the time they move forward with a background check, they've decided they want you, especially since there's a cost involved in conducting the check. So whether it's verifying your education and work history, requesting a drug test, checking your criminal history or even your credit, they're genuinely hoping that everything checks out.

When you receive an offer that's contingent on a background check, ask directly, "I'm thrilled at the prospect of working here. What is your policy on background checks? I'd like to know what specific screenings you use and the general time frame for that process." At this point, they've said they want you, so you're in a good position to ask such a question. Most employers will gladly walk you through their process.

SPEAK UP WITH CONFIDENCE

If an employer says the background screening includes a credit check—and you've seen the negative activity on your credit report—then you should consider speaking up now. You can say, "I'd like to tell you in advance what you're likely to find on my personal credit report. Please allow me the opportunity to explain it, too." It's important to have a solid rationale. Maybe you hit a challenge because of an unexpected layoff, a divorce, a medical necessity, or a problem with your mortgage—none of which are uncommon in a challenging economy. Maybe there are mistakes on your report that you're working to fix. Be prepared with a clear, confident explanation—one that you've rehearsed. Speaking up at the right moment can make or break the job opportunity.

Picture Your Success

I've talked about a lot of tough situations in this chapter. Now you know it's possible to break through the barriers that have been holding you back from achieving your goals.

Think about creating what I call a "Career Vision Board," a collage of words and pictures that reflect what you want most professionally for yourself in the next three to six months. Interior designers, film directors, and many others go through this exercise to help them visualize the look, mood, and tone of their projects. By making a vision board for your career, you can do the same thing. No, it won't get you the job, but it will serve as a touchstone when you're losing energy or feeling defeated after a tough day of job hunting. Plus, as you learned in the very first chapter, without the right attitude, nothing is possible.

Here's how to do it:

1. Write down three career goals, along with at least 10 adjectives that describe the attitudes and attributes you value. If you can come up with more adjectives and phrases, that's great.

2. Select an object to decorate. It should be something you can look at daily. When I make vision boards, which I tend to do every other month, I use large glass dishes, which sit on my desk and are hard to miss. For less than a dollar you can buy a wood door hanger or box at a crafts store. You can use poster board. The larger the object, the more time you'll invest in creating the perfect finished product. Craft shops, discount housewares stores, or even your own closets and cabinets will turn up inexpensive or free items.

3. Buy Modge Podge craft glue or use watered-down Elmer's glue. (Optional: Mix in a very small amount of glitter for a fairy dust effect.) Grab a paintbrush, too.

4. Cut out words, photos, sentences, quotes, designs, and more from magazines, newspapers, or other documents that speak to the points you listed in step 1. You can also print similar stuff from the Internet. There's no wrong word or wrong source for collecting materials. Feel free to include a personal photo or two for an extra touch.

5. Now start gluing it all together. Because I use a glass dish, I attach the pieces of paper to the bottom side—facing up— which means putting glue on the front of each image. If you're using a box or poster board, you'll put glue on the back of each image instead. Don't be shy about overlapping. There's no right or wrong way to do this. It's all about your vision. Just be patient as you fill in all blanks. If there are holes to fill, go back to those stacks of magazines. Every spot should be taken for the best effect.

6. Put the finished object in a very prominent place where you'll see it daily. Ideally it'll go in a spot where you see it for a large chunk of your day, such as on your desk, next to your bed, on your kitchen counter—you get the idea.

7. Invest just two minutes a day—come on, even the busiest among us can spare two minutes—holding your project and reflecting on one or two of its messages.

Ready to sit down with your dish or board, that stack of magazines, and a pair of scissors and get super creative? Listen to Bruce Springsteen's "The Rising" and Corinne Bailey Rae's song "Put Your Records On" and be inspired to pursue your dreams.

CHAPTER 6

Power in Numbers

Band together with others in a job club

Job hunting can be lonely. And that loneliness, especially when everyone you know seems to be running to meetings or knee-deep in projects with no time to chat, can be very defeating. You have to shake it off in a positive way. One of the best ways is to connect with other job hunters in a job club.

I launched a national job club initiative online at the ABC News website (ABCNews.com/JobClub). We've been wowed by the success. Job clubs have sprouted up all over the country, giving hope and solidarity to people looking for work.

WHAT'S A JOB CLUB?

A job club is a support group where you can share contacts and job leads, brainstorm for new ideas, and offer much-needed camaraderie to keep everyone's spirits up. Think about it like a book club, but instead of talking chapters, you're focused on careers. Money clubs were once popular where members worked together to make joint investments. We also know that trying to lose weight is easier when you do it with a buddy. The same is true on a job hunt. Victory is easier when you're accountable to a team that's truly rooting for your success rather than trying to go it entirely alone.

Club members help one another stay positive during the job search. The club is a safe haven where everyone can practice interview skills, find a second set of eyes to look over a résumé and cover letter, get feedback on an interview outfit, and even share candid frustrations about not getting responses to applications. It's a great place to find a buddy to attend career fairs with, to share leads on potential jobs, and to meet for dinner (or just coffee or dessert for a less-expensive alternative) or to simply take a brief break from the job hunt grind. You can invite expert guests to speak to your club to offer advice on any number of subjects. Just a few hours a week can make all the difference in club members' lives, attitude, and energy as they search. Plus, once you've found work, you can continue to make great contributions to the group—a perfect way to give back to peers in need.

> **Blah: "I'm going it alone."**
>
> **Ah!: "Teaming up with others will keep my energy high and build my network."**

1) GET STARTED BY RECRUITING MEMBERS

To get a job club going, all you need is a commitment of time and a genuine desire to succeed among a core group of goal-oriented jobseekers. Make a list of prospective members—try to keep it between 6 and 12 people so that you have a diverse group from a variety of industries and even age groups, but not too many so each member gets attention and customized advice. Widen the circle beyond your best friends, so the gatherings stay focused on work issues, rather than personal ones. List a club invitation on Craigslist, Facebook, or LinkedIn. Find online message boards for job hunters in your area and post a notice. Check with church groups to seek new members. Consider people you've met at job fairs or through an unemployment or outplacement office. Former colleagues may be able to make referrals, too. There's no shortage of people who'd welcome the chance to join your effort.

2) PICK A MEETING PLACE

Because your group may consist of strangers, you should hold your first several meetings in a public place. Agree on an easily accessible spot, such as a public library, coffee shop with plenty of seating area, or a free space in a recreation center or place of worship. If the weather is nice, you can even choose a picnic table in the park. It's easy to score a free spot for a small gathering, especially when your mission is clear. No matter what, choose a location that is mutually convenient and accessible to the majority of members. Nobody should have to make a costly drive or spend tons of time trekking to the meeting spot. Be considerate about the availability of free parking, too.

3) IDENTIFY GOALS AND EXPECTATIONS

The first get-together is really a getting-to-know-you session. This is the time for everyone to agree on the club's goals after sharing individual backgrounds and professional goals with the group. It's important for everyone to feel comfortable with the overall dynamic before deciding whether or not to commit to ongoing participation. Start by going around the room and asking everyone to provide a two-minute introduction that reflects work history, the circumstances that led to an interest in this group, and up to three desired goals from the meetings. If possible, use a large white board to jot down the proposed group goals. If no board is available, keep track on a legal pad.

Once everyone has spoken, allow attendees to pose follow-up questions to each person to get an even better understanding of experiences and expectations. For example, after sharing the type of role she's looking for, questions to one woman could deal with what specifically she has been doing to find a new position in that line of work. Someone may share that he's having difficulty getting motivated, and a follow-up question could focus on how he spends his days, in an attempt to get to the root of his frustrations.

Be patient and polite to allow each person to state his case and share his experiences without speaking over him.

4) NAME IT

This is a fun part. Toss around ideas for naming your club. It'll not only instill solidarity but define the club's mission and reflect your collective personalities. I've heard of successful clubs with fun names like the Fearless, Fabulous Fargo All-Stars and groups with more serious names like the Positive Professionals of Phoenix. There's no right or wrong name; it's all about whatever works for you. Don't use lewd or inappropriate language. Settle on something that everyone will be proud to share with kids or Grandma.

5) NO COMPLAINING

Make the club a whine-free zone. Everyone there knows how tough it is to be looking for work. Use the time together more productively by focusing on the future and how to jump-start your job search. By the same token, everyone must agree that what happens in the club, stays in the club. Without a promise of confidentiality, it's impossible for attendees to be truly candid about their struggles and experiences.

6) ASSIGNMENTS FOR ALL

Each person should be accountable to the group between meetings. Assignments help fuel productivity that's needed to achieve results. It can be as simple as ticking off a target list of employers to contact or making a certain number of follow-up calls. The assignment may be research-based or involve attending career fairs. Share leads and tasks among one another and encourage each other's step-by-step success. Have everyone bring a notebook to the meeting to record ideas and leads.

7) SETTLE ON MEETING TIMES

A regular weekly or biweekly get-together at a convenient time and place is ideal because it keeps the momentum going, but, people are busy so you have to be somewhat flexible. Agree on the most convenient time and day for the majority of members. Distribute contact information of each member and establish a routine for notifying one another if someone plans to be absent. How will he or she be kept in the loop on what took place? Choose a club captain who'll create an agenda—based on members' desires—for each meeting and will help facilitate outside communication.

8) SET UP A SOCIAL NETWORK GROUP

To facilitate updates and communication among members outside of meetings, set up a private group on Facebook or LinkedIn for each member to join. Use this forum to keep one another up to speed on what you're doing—the highs and lows—between formal get-togethers. This is also a chance for members to receive feed-back and coaching from peers on what's happening that day. For example, when a member learns he has an interview scheduled, he can alert the group online and ask for help with interview preparation.

9) DETERMINE HOW TO MEASURE SUCCESS

Everyone defines success differently. Ultimately it's about each person becoming gainfully employed, but in the meantime you'll need small, measurable goals to get there. Getting a call back, making new contacts, and securing an interview may all be cause for celebration. Without recognizing these moments it's difficult to keep the group upbeat and motivated, so don't skimp on opportunities to praise each person for at least one accomplishment at every meeting. After the first few meetings, set some goals on what the long-term success looks like and when you ideally hope to get there. Keep track of the progress and revisit your plans monthly.

10) CREATE AN AGENDA

By the second or third meeting, you should be able to come up with a draft of an agenda to be followed for subsequent meetings. Going through this exercise will keep things on track and moving along, which shows respect for everyone's time. You may have all day, but another member may have other commitments. If your meetings last 90 minutes, here's a potential agenda, which you should alter to best serve your needs.

:00 to :05   Arrivals and informal greetings

:05 to :25   Two-minute updates from 10 members

:25 to :45	Follow-up questions and brainstorming on key challenges
:45 to 1:15	Guest speaker presents
1:15 to 1:35	Q&A with guest
1:35 to 1:40	Reflection on best successes
1:40 to 1:45	Distribution of assignments

Consider these job club dos and don'ts:

Do

- Invite guest speakers to join your weekly meetings. Each member should research potential guests, and one or two people can take responsibility for reaching out to secure speakers. One speaker per meeting is plenty. Among the people to consider:

  - A college student or recent grad to address social media to make sure all members are maximizing the power of these networking tools.

  - Local authors who write about business issues or personal development.

  - Career coaches, résumé writers, or outplacement specialists on job search techniques.

  - HR representatives from popular employers in your area to reveal the inside scoop on the hiring process.

  - A business writer or editor from the local newspaper to share industry trends and business insights.

- Keep all conversations confidential. Unless everyone agrees that you're using parts of the discussion for the benefit of another member, what is said in the meeting stays with the group.

- Focus on mutual support. Everyone should receive help—and give it, too. Each member must offer some form of assistance to another. This may include a contact, an idea, feedback, or moral support and genuine encouragement.

- Continue to include members who've been hired or agree to replace their spots with a new unemployed member. New perspectives and fresh blood, as they say—some the newly hired or the newly joined—will benefit the group.

Don't

- Allow alcohol. This is a serious business meeting, not a social gathering. Everyone must be clearheaded to benefit from the discussions.

- Bring extra friends or surprise guests. Job clubs aren't baby-sitting groups, nor should they be used for tag-alongs. Unless you've cleared it with the whole group, don't show up with unexpected pals.

- Exchange money. Do not charge a fee for participation or request payment for advice from members. This isn't a money-making group; it's a free support service among professionals who genuinely want to receive and give job-search assistance.

- Be rude or judgmental of members. Constructive criticism is perfectly acceptable, but harsh tones and bullying should not be tolerated among members. Everyone must enforce this and speak up if there's a violation.

Establish your own rules of engagement during the second meeting. By then everyone has introduced himself or herself and each person has had a chance to think about what he or she expects from the group. Everyone should contribute to the formation of the rules. One member can type it up and distribute an e-mail to everyone else. Remind everyone of the rules once a month or as often as you find it necessary.

There are two things you can get from a job club that you can't get from even the most understanding friends and family members. (1) Relief. You can separate your job hunt from your personal relationships, taking the pressure off yourself, your friends, and your family. Most can't really help you get a job if they haven't already, so talking about it constantly may damage those relationships. A job club gives you a sounding board that doesn't have to do the dishes with you every night. (2) Understanding. The members know what you're going through—looking for work right now, in these times—and just how tough it is. When they tell you that they get it, you know that they really do.

Once you start or join a job club, learn more about having me visit with your group. More information can be found on page 301.

So put on the classic tune "I'll Be There"; go for the Jackson 5 or Mariah Carey, it's up to you. And while you're at it, put on the Bill Withers favorite "Lean on Me." Sit down and make a list of 10 people who are out of work or post a message on Facebook calling for other job seekers to join in with you. Get the names, get together, and help one another get hired.

CHAPTER 7

The Best Thing
Next to Being There

How to get hired from home

Every day, without fail, I get an e-mail asking me for advice on how to work from home.

Perhaps you need money but you also need to be at home for your family. Maybe you're a retiree who needs a few extra dollars to make ends meet. Maybe you just want to save for something special. Maybe there are physical reasons that make commuting to work too difficult. You may also be burned out from your job search and need a brief change of pace.

Whatever the reason, working from home is the wave of the future. There are thousands of companies that currently use hundreds of thousands of at-home workers on staff or for contract work. That number will climb as technology makes it easier and more affordable for everyone to connect, regardless of physical location.

Until three years ago, I had never given much thought to the people who work from their homes every day. But I began to learn about this rapidly growing army when both Women For Hire and *Good Morning America* websites were deluged with questions about finding at-home work.

Since then, I've traveled the country connecting women with those opportunities. I learned so much about the work-at-home industry that I co-wrote a *New York Times* bestselling book called *Will Work from Home: Earn the Cash—Without the Commute,* a guide to making money at home, with Robyn Spizman. (Indulge me while I toot that horn for a second: the book also made the *Wall Street Journal* and *Business Week* bestseller lists. See, it's not so difficult to sing your own praises.) And making money from home remains a topic I am asked about frequently.

It can be a win–win situation. Businesses recognize that tapping into at-home workers has enormous benefits: no overhead and less frequent turnover. Because the majority of Americans are now online, technology has made us constantly, some would say incessantly, available. With computers and phones and webcams, there's no reason why work can't be done anywhere.

After all, if Agatha Christie could write her books while in the tub (true), there's no reason you can't work as a virtual rep in your kitchen.

But first—time to get real and . . .

Be Honest with Yourself

Do you have the temperament to work from home? It takes a self-starting, focused, and dedicated person to shut out the distractions of home and get work done.

Here's a quick quiz to see if working from home could be for you.

1. Have you been thinking about working from home for six months or longer?
   Yes _____   No _____   Not really _____

2. When you mention the idea of working from home to a friend or family member, do they say, "That sounds perfect for you!"
   Yes _____   No _____   Not really _____

3. Have you talked with anyone who works successfully from home about how it really works?
   Yes _____   No _____   Not really _____

4. When you are home alone, are you able to read an entire newspaper or magazine article from start to finish without getting distracted?
   Yes _____   No _____   Not really _____

5. Do you tackle new tasks as soon as they come up, such as organizing the carpool or planning a vacation?
   Yes _____   No _____   Not really _____

6. Do you find that you get the most done when you're home alone?
   Yes _____   No _____   Not really _____

7. Are you a to-do-list person, with a plan for whatever project you take on?
   Yes _____   No _____   Not really _____

8. Do you make most of your friends and social connections outside the workplace?
   Yes _____   No _____   Not really _____

As you might imagine, if you've answered yes to the majority of these questions, you might have the right personality for working from home. If the majority of your answers were no or not really, it probably means that you thrive on the personal interaction and structure found in a traditional workplace.

> **Blah:** "I want to work from home so I don't have to pay for childcare."
>
> **Ah!:** "Working and watching my children are major responsibilities I take seriously, so I'll have to arrange a schedule that allows me to do both, but not at the same time."

For those out there who answered yes, let's take a look at what you need to face before you get started.

GOT THE GOODS?

Obviously you will need certain equipment to do this kind of work. Each job has its own requirements, but you will definitely need the following:

- An up-to-date computer, high-speed Internet access, a landline, and a professional e-mail address.

- A quiet, dedicated workspace that's not the kitchen table.

- Defined work hours. Determine how much time you can work uninterrupted. Clients or bosses need to know when you will be available. Firm work hours can also prevent you from burning out.

KNOW HOW

If you see an ad that promises big bucks with no training or skills required, steer clear—there is no such thing as money for nothing. (More on these scams later in the chapter.) But you may have to invest and pay for training yourself. Training programs for at-home work can be found online. Pick them with care. Don't choose the program with the cheapest price tag; pick the one with the best job placement success rate for graduates. Do your own research, contacting former students or companies to find out if the program has a good reputation.

Some companies offer training that is considered an investment on your part, meaning you usually don't get paid for it. This tells the employer that you're willing to put in the time to do a good job. Just make sure there is a predetermined period for this free work.

> **Blah:** "Give me anything that's easy so I can just make ten dollars an hour from home."

> **Ah!:** "Making money is never a breeze but I have great skills to offer, and I'm going to market myself."

GETTING THE GIG

You probably won't have to interview in person, but you'll likely have a virtual interview of some sort. Treat it as professionally as if you were sitting across the desk from the decision maker—no crying babies, no dogs barking. The interviewer will judge you on your phone manner because your voice will be the face of the company.

You may be asked the following questions, among others:

What hours are you willing to work? Express a willingness to work as many hours as possible, including some time during nights and weekends. Offering to take the less-popular shifts makes you more attractive to a prospective employer. Once you've proven your abilities, you should be able to improve your schedule. But first, get your foot in the door by being flexible.

What do you do when your computer breaks down? This is your chance to demonstrate a comfort level with technology. If you're great on the phone, and you've got exceptional sales or customer service experience, but you're not so hot on the computer, fix that before applying. If you panic when your computer won't start, now is not the time to admit it. If you get flustered when too many programs are open at once, consider taking a computer course at a local community college so you can improve your online comfort level and confidence. Your answer should reveal the steps you take, such as basic trouble-shooting and an ability to move through a checklist to get up and running. This is computer-based work, so you can't overlook the importance of expressing ease with basic technology.

What's the general environment around your workspace? The company wants to make sure your answer doesn't include a crying baby or a barking pit bull. The worst response is one that reveals noise or chaos in your home. Make it clear that all is quiet while you're working and that you're prepared to focus on work during the agreed-upon hours.

For some positions, you may be asked to read a script. The decision makers are looking for enthusiasm, which can be difficult without face-to-face interaction with a customer. If you can't do it effectively, you won't get the opportunity, so practice the scripts with a friend until you get them down.

Here's an example of a script for a virtual customer service position to give you an idea of what is expected:

Thank you for calling the Auto Center. How may I help you? You are locked out of your car? Oh, I am sorry to hear that. May I ask for your membership number? Thank you, Mr. Brown. May I have the year, make, and model of your vehicle, and where you are located? A dispatcher will contact you within 15 minutes with an estimated time of arrival. Is there anything else I can help you with, Mr. Brown? Thank you for calling the Auto Center. (Courtesy of Arise Virtual Solutions.)

HOME ECONOMICS

Very few companies that use at-home workers will put you on the payroll. Instead, you'll become an independent contractor, which means no taxes will be taken out of your paycheck. You are responsible for putting away enough money to pay your income taxes come April 15.

An extra hitch: The government expects you to pay your taxes quarterly if you expect to owe more than $1,000 in federal tax in a year. A form 1040-ES and payments are due on April 15, June 15, September 15 and January 15. File on time or risk paying a penalty.

So instead of facing a big bill four times a year, you will probably want to set aside a regular percentage of your income—enough to cover state and federal taxes—in a bank account that you can't touch. You should tack on an extra 10 percent just in case you make a mistake in your math. An accountant can estimate what you'll owe and set up a timely payment process for you.

Here's a look at some of the many different kinds of at-home work available to you.

Helping Others Out—From Home

Susan Joyce was one of 120,000 people who were laid off in 1994 by the now-defunct Fortune 50 tech company Digital Equipment Corporation.

"Since my attorney husband had a good job, I didn't have any financial pressure," she says. "I was so blessed. Many others were not as lucky. The post-layoff damage to peoples' lives was enormous: One of my co-workers stabbed his wife to death and then hung himself."

Building on her experience in HR and technology, she began studying, writing, and speaking about the then-brand-new field of online job search. Before the dot-com boom, she had worked in Harvard University's personnel office and at a Boston salary survey consulting company.

Then in 1998 for $6,000, she purchased a two-year-old website, Job-Hunt.org, which now has more than 11,000 links to employers and job search resources.

"It started as my 'good deed'—paying forward to those people who weren't as lucky as I was and to others who've lost their jobs or who hate the jobs they have," Susan says.

Working mostly from home, she's earning more than $100,000 a year from advertiser-generated revenue—"more money than I ever dreamed of earning in the corporate world," she says. "I keep turning down offers to sell it. What else would I do?"

Virtually There

Virtual is a term you'll come across quite a bit when searching for the at-home jobs that require some form of interaction with customers or clients.

Virtual customer service agents are those voices you hear when you place a J.Crew order or call to book flights with Virgin Atlantic

Airlines. That voice on the other end might well belong to someone working out of his or her living room, anywhere in this country. Retailers, banks and financial institutions, restaurant chains, infomercials, airlines, and other businesses that take great pride in their customer interaction are keeping these calls on American turf instead of routing them to offshore agents.

If you've got solid customer service skills, a computer with high-speed Internet access, a dedicated land line, a workspace free of crying babies and barking dogs and at least 20 free hours a week, you could apply to do likewise. Specialized skills, such as licensed insurance brokers and bilingual (Spanish and English) expertise, are in greater demand than general customer service experience. The base pay generally ranges from $8 to $15 an hour, plus potential commission and bonuses, depending on your skill level, call volume, and assigned accounts.

To become a virtual agent, connect with one of the major players, which include Teleperformance, the world's largest call center company; Alpine Access, which hires employees; LiveOps and VIPDesk, which pay agents as independent contractors; and Arise, which requires individuals to incorporate. There are pros and cons to each business model, so visit their sites to learn which might be best for you. I've listed others in the resource section at the end of the book. Always read the fine print. In some cases, you may be required to pay for a background check before you'll be considered. That doesn't mean it's a scam; it's just the company policy, so pay attention to such details before completing applications.

If more American businesses brought their virtual call center operations back to this country, more opportunity would open up for this type of home-based work.

Virtual assistants are administrative professionals who provide support for their clients from home. That can mean everything from answering the phone to managing e-mails, word processing, updating websites, writing press material, arranging travel, and doing bookkeeping—anything a business assistant might do in an executive's outer office except fetch the coffee. But instead of sitting face-to-face with the boss, you perform your work at home. Pay ranges from $10 to $75 per hour. VANetworking, International Virtual Assistants Association (IVAA), and Team Double-Click can help you get started. It's likely that you'll have to build your own client base to generate a full-time income.

Virtual concierges provide the same kind of special treatment hotel guests receive, except they provide this customer service for clients in every kind of business. This could mean everything from making dinner reservations and arranging dry-cleaning to be delivered to sending gifts and booking vacations. Some companies even hire virtual concierges to help employees get their chores done rather than give them time off to do it themselves. Healthcare providers and high-pressure technology companies are among the more frequent purchasers of such services because their employees put in long hours in demanding roles. Pay ranges from $10 to $50 per hour, depending on location and assignments.

Maybe you'd like to be a *virtual expert*. Sites such as Elance, Guru, and oDesk connect businesses ("buyers") with independent workers ("service providers," in other words, you). They post thousands of opportunities and facilitate the whole process, from hiring to payment. They offer extensive opportunities for skilled professionals, from software developers and website designers to transcribers, writers, and publicists.

The sites allow you to create a free profile to tout your skills and experience and to take assessment tests that certify your skill level for prospective clients. You can also view postings of opportunities and bid on appealing projects, determining your own hourly or project rate. (On Elance, for example, project fees can range from $50 to design a logo to more than $10,000 to develop a website.) You may have to accept initial assignments for a low hourly or project rate, but as you gain experience and log hours in the systems, your rate will increase. This is similar to eBay in some ways: Buyers are more likely to pay more for purchases from sellers with a long track record of successful sales than from those sellers who are new to the system.

Medical coding, billing, and transcription specialists are in a growth industry, according to the Bureau of Labor Statistics. Changing regulations in healthcare and the aging boomer population means that healthcare is one of the few industries that is somewhat unaffected by the current economic woes.

Coders translate the names of diseases, ailments, and treatments into numerical codes, essential for filing insurance claims. Only about 15 percent of coders work from home.

But some 85 percent of medical transcriptionists work from home, interpreting audio files from a doctor's dictation to a proper text file for a patient's permanent medical history.

As you can imagine, you'll need specialized training in these fields. Women For Hire has done a lot of work with Career Step, which offers affordable training and, just as important, job placement assistance upon graduation. (The company also offers Legal Transcription and Pharmacy Technician training programs as well.) The Association for Healthcare Documentation Integrity (ahdionline.org) offers advice on how to choose a reputable training program, along with its recommended online schools. Do your research.

Tutoring has become an online growth industry. Some tutors work directly with parents and students, whereas others work regularly with private and public schools. Tutors specialize in subject matter or in college test prep courses. Kaplan is among those services hiring both on-site and online tutors. I've also met many teachers who make extra money through Tutor.com. Rates begin at $10 per hour. You can also build your own tutoring practice, which means lining up your own clients. You can make a higher hourly rate, depending on location and grade level.

Online guides use their expertise to assist others in need of their knowledge. About.com offers qualified applicants the opportunity to become guides if they have proven expertise in a topic area. As a guide, you're responsible for frequently publishing full-length articles and blog posts. If you go to the website, you'll find guides writing about everything from 15-Minute Fashion to 48 Hours in Vegas. About.com offers a base payment to qualified writers, with a commission based on the number and growth of page views.

In a similar vein, ChaCha.com pays real-time guides to help users search for information. Guides are paid per successful request—usually around $3 to $9 per hour. On LivePerson.com and JustAnswers.com users pay a fee for expert guides (like you) to answer their questions. You're paid per transaction based on a fee determined by you. If you're a gardening expert, a lawyer, or a TV trivia nut, this could be a way to earn some extra money.

Here are other sites to look into if you are considering working from home:

- Major online job boards: Hotjobs.com, CareerBuilder.com, Monster.com, SimplyHired.com, and Indeed.com. Use keywords like *virtual, home-based, telework,* and *telecommute* to find the openings.

- Post your job skills at these sites: Elance.com, oDesk.com, Sologig.com, Guru.com, and Craigslist.com. Employers and business owners looking for freelance help search these sites for home workers. Similarly, you can search them for opportunities that appeal to you.

With all of these sites, beware of scams. For example, on Career Builder.com, among other sites, you'll find legitimate postings, along with Google ads that often feature fraudulent home-based opportunities. Be sure you evaluate any potential opportunity before applying or sending money. While your Social Security number is required for background checks when applying for certain positions, the application process should never involve providing date of birth, bank account numbers, and personal passwords.

Here are sites that specialize in particular fields.

Medical transcription training: CareerStep.com, Ahdionline.org

Tech support: CrossLoop.com, GeekSquad.com, Computer Assistant.com, PlumChoice.com, SupportFreaks.com, Support .com

Telemarketing: TeleReach.com, Intrep.com, WestAtHome.com

Tutors: Tutor.com, TutorVista.com, ASAPTutor.com, Kaplan .com, GrowingStars.com, SmartThinking.com

Virtual customer service: AlpineAccess.com, LiveOps.com, WorkingSolutions.com, Arise.com, VIPdesk.com, Teleperformance.com, WestatHome.com

Virtual assistants and concierge services: VAnetworking.com, IVAA.org, TeamDoubleClick.com

Virtual guides and experts: LivePerson.com, JustAnswers.com, About.com, ChaCha.com

In-home care for children, the elderly, and pets: APlaceforMom .com, Care.com, SitterCity.com, Care4Hire.com, HomeInstead .com, SeniorHelpers.com, ComfortKeepers.com, SunriseSenior Living.com, Right at Home.net and FetchPetCare.com

Mystery shopper: MysteryShop.org (Don't ever pay a fee to become a mystery shopper or merchandiser. No certification is required, even though both trade groups offer such a program. No legitimate opportunity will ever require you to pay a fee to become certified or eligible.)

Merchandising: NARMS.com

Direct sales: DirectSelling411.org

Virtual travel agent: WTH.com

AT-HOME BUT OUT OF THE HOUSE

There are opportunities that allow you to get out of the house while still being based at home.

Direct Sales

Direct selling remains one of the top ways to make money outside an office or retail setting. Mary Kay, Avon, and Tupperware are the all-stars of the direct-sales game, with goods and services marketed directly to customers by independent salespeople. You get as much out of direct sales as you put into it, meaning that how much you make is in direct relationship to how much effort you devote to it. And it's not going out of style: the Direct Selling Association reports that the majority of Americans have purchased goods or services through direct sellers.

If you're interested in this type of work, consider the following issues before getting started.

IS IT RIGHT FOR ME?

Most direct sellers use the money as supplemental income, not their main source. The median income in direct sales is around

$2,500 annually, which means just a couple hundred dollars a month. Steer clear of any promise of big bucks or fast cash with minimal effort; that just doesn't exist in direct sales.

CONSIDER YOUR PERSONALITY

If you're very shy and introverted or if you're not outgoing or willing to hustle, then any form of sales probably isn't right for you. Unlike working in a retail store, where customers walk in, with direct sales you're on your own. You must go out to proactively find your customers. A driven, motivated, friendly person who wouldn't be shy about asking friends to consider making a purchase and who isn't shy about chatting up strangers, is what direct selling requires.

THINK ABOUT THE PRODUCTS

Pick a product line that you are personally passionate about. If you can't see yourself using the products or giving them as gifts, stay away.

WHAT DOES THE NAME MEAN TO YOU?

Some people prefer to go with a big name—such as Avon or Mary Kay—simply because everyone knows it, which can be comforting with sales. Others prefer to go with a name you've probably never heard of—Stella & Dot, a high-end, yet affordable, jewelry line, for example—because that too can be instrumental in generating sales. Only you can decide what's right for you and your potential customer base. Think about what your friends and people in your community are likely to buy. Consider the competition, too. If several of your friends sell a particular line now, you would probably want to pick something else so you don't face direct competition.

COSTS AND FINE PRINT

Make sure you're being asked to pay a reasonable fee to get started, including product samples, training materials—which often include manuals, videos, access to seminars, and more—plus catalogs and order forms. The median fee for a starter kit is $70, and the retail value of the products often exceeds what you're paying. Don't be sucked into opportunities that call themselves "direct sales" but require you to pay a fee solely for the privilege of becoming a seller. To pay a fee, you should be getting something tangible in return. Be sure that you're selling directly to the consumer. For example, if you're selling food products, make sure that it's food that will go right into the buyer's mouth. If you're selling cosmetics, they should be sold by you directly to the people who are putting them on. There is no shortage of scams that require you to stock up on inventory with a false promise of teaching you how to unload it to various distributors. That's not direct sales.

CHECK THE BUY-BACK POLICY

If you're not satisfied or you discover this isn't right for you, will the company buy back the starter kit? The Direct Selling Association Code of Ethics requires its 200+ member companies to buy back the kit and any product for a significant portion of the amount paid within 12 months of purchase. If the company isn't a member of the DSA, ask directly what the policy is before you make any purchases.

STILL UNSURE?

If you're thinking of signing on with a company, but aren't quite sure yet if this is right for you, contact the company and ask to attend a party in your area. See how potential customers interact with the product. If you can't attend a party, ask to talk to a couple of reps in your area to see how they're doing. Every legitimate company will gladly provide someone to answer your questions, so don't be shy.

READY TO GO?

The key to long-term direct sales success is doing at least one thing every day to build your business. To get started, make a list of 50 people you'd be excited to contact about your new product line. Begin to reach out to them with enthusiasm about your personal experience and why you think they should take a closer look at what you have to offer.

Eldercare

Eldercare can also be done from home—your client's home, not yours. Its purpose is to provide seniors with nonmedical home-based care. This work includes offering companionship, doing errands and light housekeeping, preparing meals, scheduling doctor appointments, handling bills, and other tasks family members might tackle if they were available. The pay depends on the number of hours you work and the services you provide.

Mystery Shopper

Mystery shoppers make anonymous visits to retail stores, restaurants, and gas stations to monitor customer service, the cleanliness of the environment, the availability of merchandise, and the knowledge of the sales team.

Many companies request investigations of competitors as well as their own locations, to see how they stack up. For example, you might time the wait in line at Walgreens versus CVS (two large pharmacy chains) or gauge how much a Target sales associate in electronics knows about a specific digital camera compared with a salesperson at Wal-Mart.

Never pay to become a mystery shopper. No legitimate employer will ask for a start-up or registration free. Mysteryshop.org manages a national database of companies around the country that hire shoppers.

Merchandisers

Merchandisers are hired by manufacturers to present their product in a retail environment to generate sales. You may assemble displays, distribute coupons or samples of food, restock shelves, or demonstrate products. For example, a snack company may hire you to assemble a display with a football theme around Super Bowl time. You'll have to make sure that the display is attractive, well-stocked, and placed near other products that are linked to the event, such as beverages and dips. Around the major holidays, greeting card companies look to merchandisers to visit store displays to replenish seasonal cards.

Hiring is almost always handled by a third-party vendor. Pay starts at $8 to $10 per assignment and can go as high as $30 to $50, depending on the requirements. Consider the time involved and the distance of the location to determine if an assignment is worth the money offered.

Neither mystery shopping nor merchandising provide full-time compensation. Both are ways to earn some pocket change here and there, but your bills should never depend on this kind of work.

Arts and Crafts

There are a number of online communities that function as go-betweens for artists and designers and their customers.

If you have a snazzy idea or slogan for a T-shirt, hat, or coffee mug, submit your original ideas and art online to websites like

Zazzle.com and CafePress.com You'll receive a commission whenever customers purchase items with your design, without risking a penny in start-up costs.

Etsy is one of my favorite sites; check it out and you'll see why! It is an online community that connects sellers of handmade items, including candles, clothing, ceramics, jewelry, pottery, and even food, with a worldwide audience. It's free to get started—the site takes 3.5 percent of your sales, plus a 20-cent listing fee. Each listing remains live for four months and includes up to five images along with the description.

Living the Dream

Chanel Kennebrew was working as a graphic designer but she had the soul of an artistic entrepreneur. She loved designing and making one-of-a-kind garments and accessories.

Etsy.com changed her life. Chanel has been selling her funky handmade bags and clothing on the site for just over a year. The Brooklyn-based designer, who generates thousands of dollars a year, says it's a dream come true.

"I wake up each morning doing exactly what I said I was going to do as a little kid," she says.

An added benefit: Boutique buyers and gallery owners across the country scour Etsy.com to spot new talent, which can lead to wholesale orders and showcases. In addition to shops in Texas carrying her designs, Chanel has raked in big bucks from wholesale orders from stores as far away as Japan and Russia.

"I'm not making as much as I would with a full-time graphic design position," says Chanel, "but I'm sustaining my creativity and I'm not starving."

Home-Worker Beware

There are scams out there, preying on desperate people who really need a job. You may have to pay for specialized training, but there are very few legitimate reasons to pay a company to let you work for them. For example, Mary Kay Cosmetics requires that salespeople buy a start-up kit that costs about $100. That $100 investment includes start-up supplies and training materials to get you going. It also aims to ensure that you're serious about your commitment to represent the company's product line. You can feel comfortable making that payment because Mary Kay is nationally known, has a documented history of success and a phone number you can call if you have questions. Many of these online scams have none of those.

When evaluating job postings and work-at-home ads, look for these warning signs.

- Outrageous financial claims—"Make thousands a week in your spare time." You'd do better with a lottery ticket.

- "No skills or experience required!"

- "Must act now!" "This offer expires in 30 seconds!" "Only two slots remaining!"

- Spelling mistakes and grammatical errors in the ad. When looking to make a quick buck, scam artists don't have the time to spell check.

- An e-mail address that doesn't include the company name as the primary domain. If they can't afford a website, they can't afford to pay you.

- Words and phrases such as *money transfer, wiring funds, packaging, forwarding, check cashing, lottery redemption, foreign agent,* and *overseas contact.* Those phrases are the language of a con artist. Never ever accept a check for cashing. No exceptions.

Blah: "The Internet is full of scams, so I'll never find a legitimate way to make money at home."

Ah!: "I'll do my due diligence to research opportunities to find the right one for me."

Working at home is a viable option for earning a full-time living or supplementing your income, and it's growing by leaps and bounds. It requires a great deal of focus and commitment from you. But you can do it. Play Daughtry's "Home" and Natasha Bedingfield's "Pocketful of Sunshine" and imagine the possibilities.

CHAPTER 8

Mine All Mine

The time I spent working at Nickelodeon was incredibly valuable for me. After serving in the coveted spot on the PR ladder at NBC News, where the product I was selling—network news stars—was in high demand, I really had to hustle at Nick. The consumer products division, which I was responsible for promoting at the kids cable network, was in its early days and it took a lot of work to put it on the map. The work was demanding, which enabled me to feel like my success was my own.

But after several years in the PR game, I realized I was done with the corporate world. I wanted a complete change, something more entrepreneurial. I decided to accept an offer to head marketing and public relations for a brand-new lifestyle magazine for twentysomethings owned by Ralph Lauren's son.

It was a great publication with lots of talent and enthusiasm behind it. And it was a scrappy, decidedly low-budget operation. Gone were the big expense-account lunches that I was accustomed to at Nickelodeon, no more fancy business trips. The offices were plain and cluttered—no sleek furniture or expensive art that hangs on many publishing company walls. This job was in the heart of Manhattan, and there were times when I'd hand-deliver packages on my lunch hour instead of calling a costly messenger service.

None of this bothered me. I never resented the need to be tight with a buck. In fact, I embraced it and was energized by it because it forced me to be more creative, more resourceful, and smarter about the ways I went about doing my job. I didn't have a support staff or other departments to lean on. It was up to me to make things happen.

I was now working harder than ever before and I was producing great results. It felt fabulous to help the magazine get noticed. Then it dawned on me: If I could work this hard to help someone else's dream come true, maybe I could channel all that energy and creativity into a dream of my own.

Instead of working for "the man"—or in this case, it was really the man's son—I could be the man, or in my case, "the woman." I could run my own shop, do my own thing, and pursue my own dream.

I decided to do just that. I abruptly quit, without the security of a paycheck and certainly no nest egg to fall back on. But unlike my first days at Nickelodeon, when I wanted to quit because of a fear of failure, I now quit because I felt ready for success.

There were naysayers. Most of my friends and family said, "You must be out of your mind!" With two toddlers at home, they said, I needed my steady paycheck more than ever. I was foolish to venture into the unknown.

It's important to solicit the advice of others when making a big life decision, people whose wisdom and counsel you respect. But one of the worst positions to be in is allowing yourself to be paralyzed with indecision because of the conflicting advice of other people. Risk taking is an inherent part of professional growth and success. Doing nothing, never advancing yourself, never trying to take control over your career, is a dead zone.

Reinvention: A Good Thing

A fellow entrepreneur once told Jill Tipograph, CEO of Everything Summer, a successful company that helps parents and kids find the right summer camps, that everyone should re-create themselves every 10 years.

"I think the specific time frame depends on circumstances and/or the individual, but the concept is something to aspire to," says Jill.

Jill re-created herself and founded her successful consulting practice by chance. A corporate executive, she was recuperating at home from a car accident at a time when her daughter was thinking about sleep-away summer camp.

"I applied all of my corporate, research, marketing, and client service skills to this project and saw a business could be developed helping others with this process," Jill says. "I reengineered my experience to create the entrepreneurial summer guidance business I still run today, with periodic refinements and/or extensions when I see or feel the need."

Reinvention is empowering, Jill says. "No better proof exists of your abilities and power than when you are faced with a changed path, be it by choice or force. The new you is often a better you."

I knew instinctively that going out on my own was the right thing to do. I had the energy, the desire, and an idea that I was passionate about. Risk was assuming that any employer would offer me an indefinite paycheck, especially after the experience of being fired from a job I loved. Now I preferred to rely on myself.

Remembering my interest in women's issues and my success on the high school debate team combined with my experience working in network news, helping to promote incredible women, and my all-consuming desire to run my own business—it all came together at once. I wanted to start a company to help women advance their careers in a variety of industries. Even though career fairs were a dime a dozen, nothing existed specifically for women, so I decided to create this category.

Diversity in the corporate world was a growing priority, and I thought if I could create a forum to connect smart, savvy women with some of the best employers in America, I'd have a winner on my hands. A winner for the employers, a winner for women, and a winner for me.

Now, 10 years later, Women For Hire is credited with doing just that—helping thousands of women, and even a whole bunch of great men, advance their careers.

Not that there haven't been a few bumps along the way. I had to learn, sometimes the hard way, how to run my own company.

Jump on a Good Idea

If you have a good idea for a new business, go with it, says JJ Ramberg, founder of GoodSearch.com, a search engine that raises money for its users' charities.

"Ride with the passion when you are inspired," JJ says. "Then figure out if it'll work or not."

"This is not advice meant to tell people to foolishly jump into things without thinking them through," she says. "But it is meant to say: 'Give things a chance, instead of stopping yourself right at the beginning.'"

JJ says she has always operated this way. "I've always been one to get caught up in the excitement of an idea, sign up for it, and generally it's too late to get out of it by the time I ask myself, 'What did I get myself into?' As a result, I found myself going to a college I knew nobody at, in Uganda alone working for a nonprofit, and moving cities multiple times."

When she co-founded GoodSearch in 2005, she says she jumped in head-first.

"That's not to say that I didn't eventually do all the research needed to make the company a success. I let my passion for the idea take over, which then fueled me for all the work it would take to get the company off the ground."

Because my family needed two incomes, I didn't have much time to get Women For Hire launched and making a profit. If it failed, I'd have to try to get a "real job," which of course I didn't want to do.

Instead of spending months and months crafting a business plan, I put my thoughts on one sheet of paper—a plan of sorts for my company—and dove in. I was impatient: I didn't want to talk or write about starting a business, I wanted to just do it.

My business plan outlined my goal for Women For Hire: Create opportunities for women to have successful careers by providing them with face-to-face access to employers through job fairs specially designed for women.

I went on to detail how much money I would need to get my business up an running (less than $5,000), who my target customers would be (Fortune 500 companies plus nonprofits, government agencies, and medium-size businesses), how I would reach them (cold-calling by phone and e-mail), how much it would cost to produce the job fairs (about $20,000 for the very first one), and how much profit I would need to make to keep my family fed and the business growing (this number changed all the time).

It turns out that my instinct to get going without a lengthy formal business plan was just fine. According to a 2006 survey conducted by Babson College, there was no difference in financial performance between those businesses launched between 1985 and 2003 with or without a formal business plan. It's a different story if you're looking to raise a great deal of start-up money. But if your office suite doubles as your bedroom, as mine did, and you're looking to bootstrap it, as I did, a one-pager is just fine.

I was now ready to market my services. I needed to make a splash to get my company and my idea out there.

I had a brainstorm. Star Jones was about to premiere on *The View*, so I bought 100 wholesale copies of her book, *You Have to Stand for Something, or You'll Fall for Anything*, and arranged for her to do a book signing at my very first event. I also formed a marketing partnership with *Mademoiselle* magazine, allowing them to distribute copies of the magazine and cosmetic samples from their advertisers to my career fair attendees. My event instantly benefited by the association with those two famous names—Star Jones and *Mademoiselle*—and we generated great publicity and buzz.

The first event was an enormous success. More than 1,000 women walked through our doors to connect with 50 top employers. I knew I was on to something.

Always Stay Calm: A Hot Dog Tale

"In the face of a potential work crisis, never lose your cool," says Mary Naylor, CEO of VIPdesk, an online customer service firm.

"Take a step back, take a look around, and never let them see you sweat," she says. "Even when you are literally sweating."

Her first company, Capitol Concierge, provided on-site concierge services for 80 office buildings throughout Washington, D.C. "We did anything and everything a client wanted—as long as it wasn't illegal or immoral."

One afternoon, her firm organized a baseball-themed event complete with a lobby ballpark "weenie roast" for the building owner and the 500 tenant guests. A half hour before the event, Mary discovered that the professional hot-dog cooker she had rented was on the fritz: she was about to serve hundreds of cold wieners.

"It would have been very easy to freak out, start crying, and run for the hills," she says. "Or worse, let the client know that there was a problem before it was absolutely necessary to get him or her involved."

Instead, she took a step back and tapped a few colleagues to help her out of the mess.

They found an industrial-size coffee urn in the basement that wasn't being used, filled it with water, waited for the water to boil, and dumped the dogs inside. Within minutes those puppies were hot enough to return to the professional cooker and serve.

Who knew? "More than one person said that they were the best hot dogs they had ever tasted," Mary says.

"I'm sure my client did a double-take when I came back into the room smelling like a hot dog factory with my hair dripping from my face," she says. "But I did whatever it took to make it right for the client, and I learned there is always a way to get the job done."

(And yes, Mary's client renewed the contract, and she held another weenie roast the next year.)

From our first event we (even when it was just me, in the corner of my bedroom, I always referred to "we" when discussing my business) expanded to 10 major cities, holding career expos twice a year. I started writing books, giving speeches, and building our website.

With brainstorms, however, come the occasional brain clouds. A few years ago, I read that T-shirts were not only a great marketing tool but also a way to rake in big bucks. I invested $5,000 in enough Ts to outfit an army, then customized them with designs I thought were catchy at the time—expensive rhinestones and slogans like "I bring home the bacon," and for men (yes, I made Women For Hire T-shirts for men, without the rhinestones) that read "My wife brings home the bacon." For kids, I had "My mom brings home the bacon" and "My mom works, and I'm proud of her." Another version, which became my favorite, read "I ♥ My Job."

Along with the T-shirt costs, I decided I needed professional labels—"Women For Hire Career Gear"—and we installed a customized (and, therefore, costly, at the time) shopping cart function on our website.

Cute, yes. Effective, no. In the time since my initial investment, we've barely sold $500 worth of shirts. Why? Our expertise is producing recruiting events, not making clothes.

The lesson: Stick to what you know. Just because I could sell career services didn't mean I could easily peddle clothing.

My focus, aside from that little detour, has always been to provide a top-notch service, get it out to the target audience, and sell it. If you want to start a business, that's what you should do, too.

Overcoming Job Drought

Cheryl Ludwig of Bishop, Georgia, lost her job when her former employer, a landscape nursery, laid off several staffers because of the economy. Bishop is a very small town with limited job opportunities even in good times. She applied everywhere—banks, grocery stores, retail shops, schools, government offices—you name it. Ultimately she realized that none of these places were hiring and for those that were, she faced steep competition. Cheryl found her niche working from home on oDesk.com. This work allows her the freedom to focus on her beautiful art, which she sells online through Etsy, and her reflexology, which is another passion. This, too, was an out-of-the-box solution.

If you have an idea for a business and want to give it a go on your own, now is a great time to get started. Earlier this year, in the midst of record unemployment, a Kauffman Foundation–funded U.S. Census Bureau study reported that startup companies are major contributors to job creation. The study also noted that while business start-ups decline slightly in most cyclical down-turns, start-ups remain robust even in severe recessions. If you're a bootstrapper like me, you can make a successful go of it even in bad times.

If Money Didn't Matter, What Would You Do?

Motivational speaker and consultant Jon Gordon was in sales for a technology company during the dot-com boom. He was also miserable and his marriage was falling apart.

"After an ultimatum from my wife, I knew I needed to do something different," he says. "Honestly, I prayed. I never prayed like this before. Amazingly within a week, writing and speaking popped into my head."

But while he was building his speaking and consulting business, Jon still needed to support his family, so he opened a restaurant franchise. "We put every dime we had into it and borrowed more than half to open it." Six months later, after he'd made his first profit, he began writing a free newsletter sharing positive tips. A book followed.

"I gave about eighty talks for free to get myself out there. From there I got referrals. I also went on several book tours paid for by myself and appeared on local television. All this meant that businesses started bringing me in to speak to their companies. I sold my restaurant and decided to focus a hundred percent on writing, speaking, and consulting. Then I started to consult with companies on building a positive culture at work."

His new career really took off after his book *The Energy Bus* was published. He now writes a newsletter and books, speaks and consults with businesses, schools, and professional sports teams.

"I knew this was the right path because I said to myself even if it takes ten years to become successful, this is what I truly want to build and be," Jon says. "I also knew that it wasn't about the money. I asked myself what I would do if money wasn't an issue and it would be this."

Since then, Jon has encouraged others to do the same. "It's amazing how people have found the right path and job as a result. My mission hasn't changed in the past eight years: to encourage, empower, and inspire as many people as possible, one person at a time."

Some Things to Consider

IS THE TIME RIGHT?

Do you think about your business idea 24/7? Do you wake up in the middle of the night with ideas bursting from your head? If the idea hasn't stuck with you for months, then don't rush into anything. If, however, you've been thinking about this nonstop for an extended period and you're itching to make it a reality, now may be your moment to make it happen.

ARE YOU AN ENTREPRENEUR?

Do you have the right stuff? It's a critical question because one thing is certain in business: there are no guarantees. There are a lot of risks inherent in starting a business. And it takes a lot of hard work. Most entrepreneurs start out working long, difficult hours with very little pay. You'll have to deal with risk, constant change, and long hours. You'll have to keep moving forward while constantly watching the bottom line.

So, are you a person who thrives on risk or someone who needs the security of a paycheck? If you're the latter, don't kick yourself. Running a business isn't for everyone, and it's better to know that now.

FAILURE IS A POSSIBILITY

You have to face it: More small start-up businesses fail than succeed. But that alone shouldn't discourage you. On the contrary, acknowledging the risk of failure should serve as a careful reminder not to underestimate the difficulty of starting a business. Success in business is never a given, but if you are patient, willing to work hard, and take all the necessary steps, it can be yours. And a little luck along the way certainly helps.

SUCCESS MAY NEVER MEAN SIX FIGURES

Be realistic about the financial potential of your idea. Many people start out hoping to strike it rich. Others are content to make a reasonable living. Only 3 percent of all women-owned small businesses and just 6 percent of all male-owned small businesses hit the million-dollar mark. And some 70 percent of women-owned businesses generate less than $50,000 a year, which may feel small to some, but it's just right for others.

IT'S A JOB, NOT JUST AN ADVENTURE

Owning a business isn't what you see on TV: occasional appearances at the office, all the actual work taking place off screen, and never getting in the way of long lunches and great vacations. You'd need a term beyond 24/7 to describe how hard you'll work in the real world by owning your own shop.

You're the employer and employee all in one and it will be up to you to organize your time and follow through on details. Some people burn out quickly from carrying all the responsibility for success on their own shoulders. Running a company can wear you down; a healthy enthusiasm will help you survive slowdowns.

You have to be a visionary, a diplomat, a decision maker, an office manager, and a financial whiz, or you have to know where to find these people. You have to have faith and confidence in yourself, but also the wisdom to know when to seek advice.

IT TAKES A VILLAGE

Even though you're going out on your own, you are not doing it alone. Starting a business, especially the first few years, can be trying on family life. Financial difficulties can arise until the business becomes profitable, which could take months or years. In some instances you may have to get used to a lower standard of living in the short-term. Family members must understand what to expect, and you need to be able to have faith that they will support you during hard times.

Following Her Heart

With economics degree in hand, Jessica DiLullo Herrin was about to become an investment banker in New York—her first real job.

But there was a little problem.

"I didn't remotely want to be an investment banker," she says. So, on a whim, she flew to Texas to meet with a start-up software company run by several inexperienced kids who wanted to do big things. It paid off.

"After that interview, I was so excited about the potential of the company, about the unknown upside and about my ability to make a big impact. But, it was risky, in a place where I knew no one and certainly not the beaten path. On the way back to the airport, the cab driver said to me, 'What's the best-case scenario in either path and what's the worst-case scenario? Now the one with the best-case scenario: Is it worth risking the downside?'"

Jessica says that the cabbie's questions told her that she was perfect for the start-up.

"I realized that the worst-case scenario was that I could just go back and become an investment banker," she says. "In that moment I knew I was just wired to take the path with the biggest potential upside, no matter how hard the journey or big the risk. I just thrive on hope."

That start-up was a success as are two others that Jessica founded—WeddingChannel and Stella & Dot, a rapidly growing jewelry social-selling company.

Jessica says that she has always listened to her heart to find what's right for her. "If you start measuring your net worth in life experience and happiness, you may just find that it naturally matches the career path that will also lead to financial success."

Intrigued? Great, keep reading.

HOME IS WHERE YOUR BUSINESS IS

I started Women For Hire from a corner of my bedroom, which saved an enormous amount of money on rent, utilities, and all sorts of overhead. That was a good thing because I didn't have the money to spend.

Several people told me it would be unprofessional and unrealistic to assume that the large employers that I was targeting as clients would be comfortable sending payment to my home address. Turns out not a single one questioned it. (Perhaps it's because I indicated

"Third Floor" instead of "Apartment 3A" as the payment address on invoices.) You can also rent a post office box as a mailing address and hire a service to handle your incoming calls.

NETWORK

Build a great website. Every business today—even those that don't sell anything online—should have a website. Whether you're opening a nail salon, running cooking classes from home, or promoting your PR services, you need a basic site that touts who you are and what you offer. Today everyone searches for businesses online. Restaurants, tutors, shoe repair shops—every business must be accessible on the Internet.

I cringe when thinking back to starting Women For Hire with an AOL address. It's a miracle anyone took me seriously. Having a professional e-mail address and website is as inexpensive as $10 a month, and it's the difference between *Blah* and *Ah!*

> Blah: "I have no technical skills and I'm intimidated by the idea alone of creating a website."
>
> Ah!: "If I can send e-mail and shop online, then I can follow step-by-step tutorials to build a basic website to support my business."

NO MONEY DOWN

Figure out how to get your business going with as little money as possible. People tell me all the time that they have a great idea, but they lack financing to get it off the ground. Although some businesses need capital to get started, many can be launched on a shoestring especially if you're determined to make it happen.

The upside of using your own money—a home equity loan, savings, or even low-interest credit cards: You run the show, and all the profits, if there are any, are yours. Unfortunately, you're also on the hook for all the money, which means you may be risking a lot of personal debt.

Perhaps family and friends can help you with loans. If you go that route, draw up a contract and make it clear so everyone knows what to expect. Don't lose sight of the personal risk either: If you don't succeed, it's Mom's or Uncle Joe's money that you're losing.

You can also use the church raffle model, though it may be easier said than done. Ask a number of people for a small amount of money to get you going. Have a gathering to present your idea to 50 friends and ask them each for $100. That will net you $5,000 in start-up cash at low risk to those investors. It's probably not easy to find those 50 pals, but look at your contact list and see who might share your vision and have a small amount of money to spare. Maybe you only need $500 for the basic start-up supplies and you can ask five people for $100 each, or 10 people for $50 each. Sometimes presenting them with a reason to believe in you and your idea, such as a testimonial from your first client or your first completed project, will make it easier for them to open their checkbook. Many may also view it as a goodwill gesture—a donation to a friend's cause for the price of a nice shirt or a really good meal. They hope you'll remember them when you strike gold.

Prosper.com, VirginMoneyUS.com, Loanio.com, and Lending Club.com are peer-to-peer lending sites that you can review when looking for loans or start-up money.

Blah: "I could never afford to start a business, and I won't qualify for a bank loan."

Ah!: "Women excel at bootstrapping, and I'm going to make this work with minimal resources because I want it badly."

Grants are few and far between unless your business is closely aligned with a cause earmarked for grants. You can find out about grants at the Small Business Administration website (sba.gov) or SCORE (score.org).

TEAMWORK

In the very early days of Women For Hire, I had no money to hire staff. My business was growing but not enough to pay employees. But that didn't mean I could go without the help. I relied on free-lancers and family members to pitch in.

Another avenue—internships. Initially, I assumed that college students would be interested in working only for big-name companies that would give their résumés a wow factor.

Then I posted internship opportunities on college message boards, offering real hands-on experience, a chance to pitch ideas to the boss (me), and business experience to rival any lessons learned in the classroom. It was as if I had won the lottery. Many talented, creative people were eager to cut their teeth on my dream.

Contact schools in your area to offer prospective interns the chance to help with your start-up.

Blah: "This won't work because I have no money to hire a staff, and I can't do all of this stuff myself."

Ah!: "I need help, so I'm going to get an intern from the local community college, and I'll ask friends and family to pitch in. I know they support my dream and would gladly help if asked."

I'LL TRADE YOU

When I needed professional help from an accountant and a web designer, I was clear that I had just about no money to spend, but that I was building a big business. I'd be a long-term client if they took me under their wing on reasonable terms. In some cases, I bartered a booth at my career fairs or my career coaching services in exchange for someone else's expertise. Other times, I paid a reduced rate with promises of future business. True to my word, I stuck with the first accountant for six years until I hired someone internally, and I continue to work with one of our original webmasters.

That said, there are two areas in which you cannot skimp—legal and tax advice. If you can't find someone who will work with you on price, find a way to pay for this expertise. The cost of making a mistake in either of these areas could cost you your business and seriously affect your personal finances.

Think About Your Next Move

Nell Merlino, founder of the nonprofit women's entrepreneur group Count Me In for Women's Economic Independence, says she used to worry about finding the right job and fitting in.

"It wasn't until I had my own business that I finally felt that I love what I do every day," says Nell, author of *Stepping Out of Line*.

After working for others for 15 years, Nell says she was bored, underappreciated, or too often running into trouble with higher ups. It wasn't until the end of working on Michael Dukakis's 1988 presidential campaign that she got the idea that she might be an entrepreneur.

"I had run advance teams all over the country, including one that organized a rally with forty thousand people in forty-eight hours," Nell says. "The thought of looking for yet another job where I would crack my head on that glass ceiling was so unappealing."

Around that time, a good friend had started a consulting practice and had more business than he could handle. Nell took over one of his contracts. "I found that I loved being in charge of my own schedule, marketing my skills and talents, and being my own boss."

That was November 1988.

Nell has worked for herself ever since, creating memorable strategic campaigns like Take Our Daughters to Work Day.

In 1999 she founded Count Me In, which helps empower women entrepreneurs. The group launched Make Mine a Million $ Business Race (makemineamillion.org) to inspire and guide thousands of women in a year-long business growth marathon to find and grow the entrepreneur in them.

As you think about your next move or are forced to look for a new job, Nell says you should explore all the different work possibilities: corporations, public-sector institutions, nonprofits, entrepreneurial organizations, small companies, or your own business.

Small businesses employ 50 percent of the nation's workforce. "In times of recession, it is often small businesses that have the innovation, creativity, and flexibility to create fascinating jobs," she says.

PUBLICIZE YOUR BUSINESS

Nobody will share your level of passion for your business, which makes you its best advocate for promotion. Before investing a penny in paid PR services, focus on free ways to draw attention to your business.

As mentioned in Chapter 3, social networks like Facebook, Twitter, and LinkedIn are ideal outlets to reach the masses. Niche sites like Yelp, JoinSlingshot.com and Craigslist enable you to target prospective customers at no cost. Women entrepreneurs can join support groups like Collective-E and MakeMineA Million.com.

Ask complementary businesses to cross-promote services. For example, if you're starting cooking classes for kids, visit local kids clothing and shoe stores, nursery schools, and pediatricians offices. Offer to promote them on your website and to your clients if they do the same. Prepare a flyer to leave in their lobby or to post on their bulletin boards. Suggest doing a kid's birthday party using your classes as the main activity.

Recently I was asked by a woman with a new pet massage business how she might spread the word quickly. I suggested partnering with the most popular pet store in her area to host in-store events every Saturday where owners could bring their animals for on-the-spot mini massages. It's good for the store because it brings new and existing customers into the shop, and it's good for attracting awareness and customers for this new pet massage business. Following this advice has enabled her to build a client base to get her business off the ground.

BECOME A MEDIA DARLING

You don't have to start your media campaign on network TV or *Newsweek*. Think local TV, radio, and newspapers. Make a cold call to get the name of the appropriate producers or writers, then send a well-crafted pitch. Announce your business, declare your expertise, and give three to five solid reasons why someone should interview you. Don't overlook blogs and websites; some draw more eyeballs and business than their print counterparts.

Subscribe to HelpAReporter.com, which delivers a free daily e-mail with lists of urgent queries from journalists looking for expert sources and story ideas. You can respond on your own, without paying for the services of a pricey publicist.

GET CREATIVE WITH YOUR PR PITCH

Back to the kids' cooking classes. Instead of simply saying, "I'm starting classes for kids, and I could really use some publicity" (yup, you guessed it, that's a *blah*), your pitch turns to an *Ah!* when it's timed to a holiday, such as five simple ways to involve your kids in Thanksgiving meal preparation. Maybe it's five unique Valentine's treats to make with your kids. Do your homework; find out what kind of segments the television show runs or explore the type of events a local business plans, and tailor your pitch to fit in with that format, adding your personal twist. For example, if you've noticed a lot of segments or events on saving money and penny-pinching, include that in your pitch. You could offer "Three healthy meals to make with your kids for under five bucks!" Who wouldn't snap that up? Spend a week carefully watching segments on the show you want to pitch. Make note of the structure of the content of each segment, then mirror your pitch to that format.

Give—And You'll Get

"You have to view the press as a pro bono opportunity," says Gary Schatsky, president of ObjectiveAdvice.com, a fee-only comprehensive financial adviser. When he opened his business, Gary called radio stations and landed a weekly show.

"I believe in what I do. I had a product that's not readily available to most people, financially or geographically, so I saw the show as a way to get the message out. I knew I was doing something good, and any business that came from it was gravy."

As his radio show grew in popularity, Gary also offered himself as an on-the-record and background source for television and newspapers, developing rapport with reporters, who spread the word about his expertise. Appearances on every major network helped his business take off. "I started getting new business and enhanced how I was perceived by existing clients, but my media exposure had to reach a critical mass before I saw real results. My new clients often say they saw me on TV. Now I send out weekly updates to clients and others in my field to keep them posted on what I'm doing."

If you're not comfortable in the media spotlight, there are many other ways to share your expertise to build your business. Chair an industry committee; contribute to a newsletter; blog about your company; and keep your LinkedIn, Facebook, and Twitter profiles and postings up-to-date.

ASK FOR HELP

You can get free or low-cost business advice from professionals. SCORE (score.org) and the Small Business Association (sba.gov) have listings of counseling and assistance programs as well as government-contracting opportunities, SBA-backed loans, training programs, and grants. Both offer one-stop-shopping for fledgling business owners. Use these services.

Also, you should contact your local Chamber of Commerce to find out what licenses or certifications you may need to operate your business.

I couldn't have predicted the rich rewards (and major head-aches) associated with entrepreneurship. There's no greater professional accomplishment I could imagine for myself than having a business that does good (helps people with their careers) and does well (turns a healthy profit).

So if you have a product or service idea that you know could catch on, go for it. Crank up the Rolling Stones' "Start Me Up," John Lennon's "Dreamer," or Natasha Bedingfield's "Unwritten" and start dancing around the room and imagining your business in action and on the rise.

thanked the mayor for her time and for sharing her wisdom. Then I politely disagreed with everything she said about money.

In a perfect world, we'd all do what we love and the money would flow effortlessly into our hands. But the real world doesn't work that way. Money is a huge reason why we work; it might not be the only reason, but it's certainly close to the top of the list. We can't afford to cheat ourselves out of a single penny for our hard work.

> Blah: "There's no chance they're going to say yes, so I'm not even going to ask."

> Ah!: "If I don't ask, there's no chance they'll say yes because they don't even know what I want."

Yes, I talk the talk . . . but I've stumbled when I've tried to walk the walk.

I had always been a really big fan of *Good Morning America*, and so in 2004, when one of the producers asked me to appear on the show to do a career-related segment, I was thrilled at the chance. It went well, so I was invited back again and again. At some point, a few of the staffers there began whispering in my ear, "When are you going to become official? When are you going to become an actual contributor?" And when I asked what that meant, they all said, "You'll get paid!"

Initially I thought, Wow, wouldn't that be great? But very quickly that changed to, "Maybe I shouldn't rock the boat. You've got this good little gig going, don't get greedy and spoil it."

Hello? I would never let anyone I was coaching get away with that kind of talk. Yet, I was afraid that someone would hear my request for compensation and slam the door. Or worse, laugh at me.

I imagined them snickering, "Give that girl a little airtime, and now she wants cash, too. I don't *think* so."

I realized I had to snap out of it. A workplace expert can't shy away from one of the most important aspects of her field—pay. I had to walk my talk.

A little homework revealed that there were others on the show who were being paid to appear and offer their expertise. They had the title *contributor* and were being compensated for the time and talent they brought to the program. I knew I deserved the same, and it was up to me to ask for it.

My first step was to anticipate the opposition. Why would the executives say no to my request, and how could I respond to change their minds? You always want to go through the exercise of playing devil's advocate, to figure out all the reasons why somebody might say no.

Here's my list:

- "We haven't known you long enough."

- "We're still looking at other people."

- "We can't afford it."

- "You're not worth it."

- "We'll need time to make such a decision."

That devil's advocate is a tough customer, but I was ready for him. I carefully crafted responses to everything on the list. I was ready.

I took a deep breath, picked up the phone, and called the executive producer. I told him why I was calling and before I could even start the heavy-duty pitch, he interrupted me with, "Done."

Just like that, I became the official workplace contributor on *GMA*. Now, I'm able to get the word out about workplace issues that mean a great deal to me and positively impact people who seek to improve their working lives. Everyone at the show, starting with the anchors, is passionate about workplace issues, so I'm allowed to tackle a range of valuable topics.

Ironically, one of my most memorable segments was on negotiating. There's a brilliant professor at Carnegie-Mellon, Linda Babcock, who has done fascinating research on negotiating using the word game Boggle.

We asked Professor Babcock to re-create her research for a behavior lab segment. We posted signs on a college campus inviting anyone to participate in an experiment with the game Boggle. For their time, they would be paid between $5 and $12.

On the day of the behavior lab, the subjects filed one at a time into the room and played a round of the game. Unbeknownst to the players, they were being filmed by secret cameras as I watched from behind a two-way mirror.

After each person was done, the administrator thanked him or her and said, "Here's your $5, is that okay?"

The men generally said no, it's not okay. They wanted the $12—the top fee offered in the ad. The administrator tried to talk them down, but the men were firm.

What do you think the women said when they were offered five bucks for playing the game? Think they asked for more?

I know what you're thinking.

Sadly, you're right: The majority of the women didn't ask for more. They didn't even question why they were being offered the lowest fee. They simply accepted it with thanks.

After each one of the participants walked out of the lab, we told them they were part of a negotiation study. I sat down with each person to talk about what happened. With the men, my very first question was, "Why did you negotiate?"

I kid you not, most of the guys looked at me as if I had asked,

"Why did you put your pants on today?" Arriving naked wasn't an option, just as they never considered not negotiating. It simply wasn't an option. They were entitled to more money, so they asked for it.

The women's responses struck a chord with me. When I asked why they didn't negotiate, they said they didn't want to rock the boat or argue. Worse, they figured that the administrator didn't think they were worth more money. Some even said it wasn't a big deal because they didn't need the money.

This is what so many of us, me included, say to ourselves when faced with negotiating for something at work. We don't want to rock that boat or cause a problem or upset anyone. Instead, we are willing to just do without.

The reality: negotiation is not about arguing. It's about getting fair compensation for the work you do. Every one of the women in the behavior lab left saying, "I will never make that mistake again."

We may know we should ask for more money. It's another thing to actually speak up when you're offered a job or to knock on the boss' door and do it. But you can and you should. You owe it to yourself.

Blah: "I'll just get in there and do a good job, and then they'll pay me what I'm worth."

Ah!: "I'll point out my superior job performance to my boss to get what I'm worth."

Get the Salary You Ask For

Here are tips on how to get the right starting salary or the raise you deserve.

IT'S YOUR DUTY

You have to be compensated fairly. You may never feel comfortable talking about money. Men tend to equate negotiating with competitive sports—something they actually enjoy.

Women, on the other hand, think of negotiating as something akin to root canal. Even though it implies excruciating pain, it's not a bad analogy. If you knew your tooth was rotting, would you ignore it? Even though you might not want to get in that chair, you would definitely go to the dentist. Approach negotiating the same way. It may not be fun, but it's necessary.

WHAT DO I WANT?

Many men say that in business, money is how you keep score. In other words, the size of your salary directly relates to your value to your company. There's something to that, but I would swap out the words *money* and *salary* with *compensation*. Compensation can mean cash or some other perk that makes up for a smaller salary. In the simplest terms, it's what you want in exchange for the work you do.

In any salary negotiation, you want to go in with a list of four or five priorities—the things you want to get out of the job. At the top of most of our lists is more money. But it's important to have other options on your list, especially in a declining economy, when so many people are losing their jobs. You may hear that more money is not an option. Instead of leaving the negotiation empty-handed, continue down your list to your other priorities.

Maybe it's the ability to work from home or it's tuition reimbursement for some courses that you want to take. It could be a better title, more paid vacation time, or covering your commuting costs. The priorities will be different for each person, and depending on the particular situation that you're in, all of your wants should be—and are—negotiable. (If one of your priorities is a flexible work arrangement, see Chapter 10 for some negotiating ideas.)

So take a moment now to make a list of the top five things you would want in compensation for your work, five things that would improve the quality of your life. (Be realistic, please. I'm not talking about winning the lottery here or having a chauffeured Bentley taking you to and from work each day.)

1. _____

2. _____

3. _____

4. _____

5. _____

This list is especially important in the event the company says the offer is firm and the salary is non-negotiable. This may be true in times of economic crisis as well as for uniform positions such as training programs or all entry-level hires. In those cases, you might not have any ability to negotiate. But if the position falls outside of those categories, then you'll want to ask about the issues on your list. The company might not be able to budge on salary, but they might consider extending the number of vacation days or covering the cost of some classes for you.

ACCENTUATE THE POSITIVE

Along with your list of things you want, you have to be prepared with reasons why you deserve more compensation. Grab your "I

Rock" file and make a list of tasks associated with your position and a list of your accomplishments in the past year. Have you landed a big account? Discovered a mistake in the books that saved the company a lot of money? Taken on more responsibilities? Your "I Rock" file will help you here.

If you're new to the company, use your "I Rock" file to remind the boss what you bring to the table, such as experience, contacts, and an established track record of success.

A few years ago, *Glamour* magazine set me up with a group of women who felt they deserved more money. One of the women was a young administrative assistant at a photo agency. Within the first eight months that she was there, a colleague left, and she was expected to pick up the slack and take on both jobs. She feared that it was too soon to ask for a raise, even though she was doing the work of two people.

It was clear that the agency had confidence in her because it gave her the extra duties. Detailing all of her hard work and how she leaped into action when the company was short staffed, her "I Rock" file was filled with notes about giving her all when the company needed her most.

I advised her to repeat the word *fair* in the meeting with her boss, as in, "I know it's been hard to fill the other job, and because I've spent the last several months successfully working to carry out the responsibilities of that position, I'd like to be compensated *fairly* for my contributions."

The fair-raise pitch worked. She received a 7 percent raise and a $500 bonus. Shortly thereafter, the boss hired a second assistant. She got a raise and the help she needed because she asked for it.

Right here, list five reasons why you deserve increased compensation.

1. _____

2. _____

3. _____

4. _____

5. _____

ANTICIPATE THE NEGATIVE

That tiny voice in your head that makes you feel low, that holds you back, may finally be useful right now. Ask that little naysayer why the boss would say no to your request for better compensation. Don't let this list depress you; it's a tool to make you feel more self-assured in the room on the big day with the boss.

> **Blah: "There's no room in the budget for it."**
>
> **Ah!: "Can we make the increase part of my year-end bonus? Or can we agree that this increase will be included in the next budget?"**
>
> **Blah: "Your salary history doesn't dictate a higher starting salary here."**
>
> **Ah!: "My job and the challenges and goals I am expected to meet warrant a higher base salary." Or "The company has doubled in size since I first joined, but my salary didn't grow along with it even though it should have."**

You get the idea. Think about your situation and think of the *Blahs* and come up with some good *Ahs!* in reply.

1. **Blah:** _____

_____

1. **Ah!:** _____

_____

2. **Blah:** _____

_____

2. **Ah!:** _____

_____

3. **Blah:** _____

_____

3. **Ah!:** _____

_____

4. **Blah:** _____

_____

4. **Ah!:** _____

_____

5. **Blah:** _____

_____

5. **Ah!:** _____

_____

KNOW YOUR MARKET VALUE

You have to know what your peers are earning before you ask for a raise or accept the starting salary offered at a new job. There are several online tools, such as Salary (salary.com) and PayScale (payscale.com), that provide information on the salaries in various industries. You can also find the numbers on some industry websites or job boards. If you're a recent college grad, ask your school's career service offices for starting salaries in your field. The Bureau of Labor Statistics (bls.gov) offers data, too.

Factor into the number the size and location of the company as well as your level of experience and education. Consider economic conditions, too. Data from 2006 or 2007 aren't going to be relevant in 2009 and beyond.

You also have to read the situation accurately. It's essential to negotiate based on the relevancy of the position. For example, when you respond to an ad for a cashier's job at a hot dog joint, it's irrelevant that you're a CPA. The job pays only $10 an hour, and it doesn't require your fancy accounting expertise.

You can also ask the interviewer where the salary being offered falls in relation to what others in similar positions at the company are being paid. Sometimes this information won't be provided. Avoid getting defensive if they say it's confidential.

You can hit the phones to ask friends and peers what the going rate is for the job. Some may be reluctant to tell you, others may overstate their salary. Get as much information as you can and figure out the average. Even still, take it with a grain of salt.

All of this salary information arms you with the knowledge you need to have an intelligent conversation.

Another example from the *Glamour* gals. One of the women was a software developer making $65,000. She knew she was making less than others in her field, and her boss promised to reconsider her salary at the end of the year. At that time, she completed a job that only she had the technical skills to handle. But the boss dropped the ball and didn't give her the raise.

Like so many women in this situation, she was nervous about rocking the boat. But this is business, not personal. She had to muster up her courage and ask for more money.

She researched her market value and wrote down her talking points for her meeting with the boss, including her work that saved the day with an important client. She rehearsed her pitch to calm the butterflies in her belly and then finally sat down with the boss. Not only did she get a 7 percent raise—double the national average—but she also got a $5,000 bonus.

Here's another of my favorite stories, about a woman who stood up to a boss who kept making promises of raises he didn't keep. The heroine? My mom, Sherry Beilinson

When I was a kid, my mother managed a popular children's wear store in Miami owned by her uncle. After working at the store for years, she finally got the courage to ask for a much-deserved raise. Her uncle promised to make it happen.

Weeks and weeks went by and her paycheck remained the same, even as her patience wore thin. A couple months later, she asked him what was taking so long. His response: "Don't worry. Slowly but surely you'll get an increase."

Even though she's not one to make waves or engage in confrontation, that response didn't sit well with my mom. Always quick on her feet, she said, "I'd like to see a lot less slowly and a lot more surely." Go mom! It worked.

NEGOTIATE AS IF IT WERE FOR A FRIEND

Women are awesome when it comes to asking people to make donations to charity. Women have no trouble haggling at a flea market or demanding the best for their kids, but it's often a different story when it comes to taking care of themselves. If that sounds like you, then pretend you're speaking up for your best friend, your daughter, or the person you care most about in the world. You know you'd want him or her to get the most, so you're likely to do an effective job.

On Asking for More Money

Christine Hassler is good at helping other women solve their work-life issues, which is why she succeeds as a California-based life coach for twentysomethings.

But she has been less than stellar at asking clients for more money and increasing her rates.

"I was scared to raise my fees," Christine says. "I feared how clients would react, and rather than take the risk of losing a client, I continued to keep my hourly rate at a place that was basically cheap. I was also scared that I would not attract new clients at a higher rate."

To deal with her problem, she focused on the value she provides clients—and away from the fee she charges them.

"I was too fixated on a number rather than the quality of service I provided," she says. "I asked myself, 'Do I know that I provide exceptional value to my clients?' The answer was yes, so then the next question I had to ask was to my clients."

Instead of calling them and announcing that she was increasing her fees, Christine began conversations talking about the value they gained from working with her.

"As we began to outline the value they were receiving, it became easier to begin to speak about the fee exchange," she says.

LEAVE YOUR FEELINGS AT THE DOOR

Women often shy away from negotiating because they don't want someone to dislike them. They worry that their future employer will think, "Oh, she hasn't even started yet, and she's already demanding things."

Negotiating salary isn't about being well liked or disliked. It's about speaking up to receive fair compensation based on the position you're being asked to perform. It's not about popularity; it's about performance. Focus on the professional, not the personal.

You won't lose a job offer because you negotiate fairly. (Clearly, if you make outrageous demands that are unrealistic based on what you bring to the position, or you're not sensitive to today's economic realities, you may risk losing it. This is where research is invaluable.)

What you might not know is that the majority of employers expect you to speak up. So never mind the naysayers, do your homework, make your lists, and head into the meeting with confidence. Practice with a friend, and evaluate both your pitch and your response to a negative answer.

DON'T TAKE NO FOR AN ANSWER

If the boss won't give you more money, especially during a recession, consult your priority list and try to get something else important to you. Working from home, extra vacation days, a title, more responsibility—get something from that meeting, even if it's only a promise to revisit the situation. Ask what you need to do to get that raise and establish a mutually agreeable time frame for achieving it.

> Blah: "If they say no, I'll have to walk away feeling like an embarrassed loser."

Ah!: "If they say no, I'm prepared to offer creative ideas to see what it will take for us to come to some middle ground."

Another young woman from the *Glamour* group was a frustrated junior art director. She didn't think she would be able to improve her entry-level position for some time and was so unhappy she was thinking of quitting and starting her own firm—not a great idea so early in her career.

Together we came up with a two-pronged proposal for her boss: Promote her to the art director and give her more responsibility. Money was not even at the top of her priority list.

We rehearsed the conversation she'd have with her boss so she would be fully prepared for her meeting. She was very nervous, but ready.

Result: Her boss agreed—she got the added responsibility she wanted, *plus* a $20,000 raise for herself, which was commensurate with her new title.

All because she asked. After that exercise, *Glamour* dubbed me the "raise fairy godmother," one of the best compliments this girl could ask for.

NEVER LEAVE EMPTY-HANDED

If the answer is still a firm no, ask what you must do or what must happen to turn it into a yes. Perhaps you'll have to wait three months or you have to land a new client.

Ultimately, you will land an offer that you're comfortable accepting and when you do, take a moment to celebrate. Reflect on how far you've come to get to this point and truly savor your victory.

And take an extra moment to send an e-mail to Women For Hire so I can cheer for you, too.

No more feeling undervalued and underpaid. Do your homework to find out what others in your field are getting—both in cash and other compensation—and follow the steps outlined here to get it for yourself.

As Donna Summer sang, "She works hard for the money / so you better treat her right." Download that tune—along with Pink Floyd's "Money"—and get yourself juiced to get what you deserve. It's time to *Celebrate!* Go play some Rock Band or Guitar Hero!

CHAPTER 10

Lose the Cape, Superheroes Are a Sham

Forget balance—blend career, family, and life to get the best of all worlds

"I can't have a baby because I have a 12:30 lunch meeting."
—DIANE KEATON IN *BABY BOOM*

MOM: "You're the most important thing in the world."
SON: "No, I'm not. Your job is."
—MICHELLE PFEIFER AND ALEX D. LINZ IN *ONE FINE DAY*

Guilt, anyone? In the 1980s, women were told they had to make a choice—career or family. In the 1990s, they were told that they should try to do it all, but inevitably they'd fail.

Now, the buzzword is *balance*. Anyone can have a high-flying career and a rich family life—all it takes is organization and the ability to multitask 24/7.

Oh yes, and forget sleeping or enjoying life. Those two have to go.

I'm not a fan of the term *balance*, even though I use it out of convenience. It's an odd word to me because it implies that two things are distinct: There's work and then there's life. But for me, work is a huge part of my life. I don't try to separate my work from my life. They are completely blended together. Working full-time makes me a better mom and wife than I'd be if I were home all the time.

The happiest hyphenates I know—mother-career woman and dad-career guy—blend their lives. They do it by making tough choices, delegating, learning to say no, and redefining the *all* in "having it all."

Even though many working parents feel guilty about not spending enough time with their kids, children don't feel the same way. That's not to say they don't adore Mom and Dad. A Families & Work Institute study of more than 1,000 students in third through twelfth grades asked, "If you were granted one wish that would change the way that your mother's or father's work affects your life, what would that wish be?" A similar question asked more than six hundred employed moms and dads how they thought their children would respond. Most parents (56 percent) assumed their children would wish for more time with them. Not so, according to the kids. Only 10 percent wished for more time with Mom. Instead, 34 percent said they wished their moms would be less stressed and tired. (By comparison, 15.5 percent wanted more time with Dad and 27.5 percent wished he would be less stressed and tired.)

Have an open conversation with your kids about what they wish for you. Listen with an open mind to their responses and you may be surprised—and relieved—by what you learn.

We all have moments when we wish there were many more hours in the day. As an intense business owner, I often have difficulty understanding why my employees aren't as driven as I am at work. Why they don't think about Women For Hire 24/7 as I do. I rarely do business lunches unless I am absolutely forced to, which no doubt hinders my chance to form strong relationships. I constantly juggle dozens of tasks at once—knowing in my bones that some things suffer because my mind is racing in too many directions. My desk is a mess with piles of stuff everywhere that I promise to get to but that moment never seems to come. I let my hair go much longer than my hairdresser would like because I'm too impatient to sit for hours for a cut, color, and highlights. I often panic on Thursdays since there's only one more day in the workweek yet my To Do list hasn't gotten any shorter since Monday. To be brutally honest, there are days when I don't even allow myself to pee at work because I'm buried in typing to get it all done!

I know, I know. All of this is so trivial. Some people would love to have such "problems." But we all have moments when we wish there were many more hours in the day. We can't alter the clock, but we can explore real solutions for how to better manage our time and our expectations.

This chapter is a guilt-free zone. No "if only there were more hours in the day" thoughts allowed. We're going to explore real expectations of working parents, especially moms, and how you can accomplish them.

Kelly Ripa is one of the best blenders I know. She once told me that no childhood has ever been ruined because Mom missed a school play or a soccer game, but many jobs have been jeopardized because Mom is late too often or misses meetings. You're not a bad mother if you occasionally have to put work first.

I needed to hear this, too. I was on a business trip in Dallas when, at the end of the day, I called home to check in with my kids.

Our babysitter, Cici, answered the phone in hysterics. "911 is here. 911 is here for Jake!"

She could barely speak, so I asked her to put the paramedic on the phone. A very understanding EMT calmly explained that everything was fine. Jake had sliced his thumb climbing on a cabinet, trying to get at an antique cookie jar. The cut was very deep, ran the length of his thumb, and needed stitches.

Of course, my first instinct was to get on the next plane. The problem was that I had a huge event in Texas the next day—one that I really couldn't miss. I tracked down my husband, who took over. After a few anguished hours, I realized that Jake was not in danger, and my husband was perfectly capable of handling everything. Even though I wanted to be there, nobody *needed* me there. If I were a single mother, I may have been forced to make a different choice.

There are a number of things to take from this story.

First, after some anxious moments, I was able to delegate the situation to someone who was as capable as I am to handle it— my husband.

Second, I made a decision that was truly for the good of all of us. Earning a living to support my family was important.

Third, I worked hard to let myself off the hook. Of course, I wanted to be with Jake, and he was present in my mind every moment of the trip. Truth be told, I wanted to be needed by him. But I ultimately realized there was nothing to feel guilty about.

I travel a great deal for work and sometimes I miss school events. I've asked teachers to allow me to watch dress rehearsals if I can't be there for the big day. Our family has re-created field trips, and we've had our own sing-alongs—all of which form lasting memories. My family knows I adore them. I'm confident that I'm setting a good example for my children.

Let's be clear: I'm not saying work should always take the place of parenting or care giving. Sometimes you have to make tough choices and something's got to give. You have to be able to accept that simple truth or else guilt will drag you down. That emotion will stop you in your tracks, zap your spirit, and drain you of energy better spent elsewhere.

This is another reason why the word *balance* bugs me. Dividing time between your family, your work, and yourself will never ever be in perfect balance. Let go of that aspiration for things to be even-steven.

This isn't limited to moms: Now more than ever, working dads share in parenting duties and are eager to be active participants in their kids' lives.

Finding a Way

Take a look at your personal life and see how and where you can afford to make more use of your time.

While it'd be cool to be a super parent, it's also awfully fun to be a sane mom or dad. Consider these subtle differences:

- Stand in the kitchen all night for the bake sale vs. contribute store-bought treats.

- Car pool with friends vs. sole chauffeur for the neighborhood.

- Cheer from the sidelines vs. coach the team.

Even though one column will be perceived as going the extra mile, nobody could argue that both types of parents aren't committed to their kids.

BUILD A DREAM TEAM

Parents should create a dream team, the folks who may be able to pick up the slack when you need it. Family, friends, neighbors, church peers, domestic employees; find people you can depend on and let them help you get the job—both at home and at work—done.

I am a very lucky girl. My husband sees marriage and parenthood as a two-person job. We've enlisted wonderful women as babysitters who, in our absence, care for our kids as if they were their own. Our extended families would drop everything at a moment's notice if we needed them. I also have friends I can rely on in an emergency. I am not obsessive about my home, but I find time to keep it (relatively) clean and in order. When a big clean is needed, all of us pitch in to make it a group effort.

This dream team makes my life possible—my life as a wife, mother, and career woman. They also release me from the tension of trying to get it all done. It's hardly stress free, but I don't experience the outright panic of not being able to do it all.

Not convinced you can do it, too? Read on.

DELEGATE AT HOME

At some point you have to admit to yourself that you can't do it all alone, that you need help. Studies at Oxford University and the University of Michigan found that people of all ages perform tasks more precisely and expediently when they don't try to tackle many tasks at once, but do one at a time.

I remember hearing bestselling author and life coach Cheryl Richardson talk at a women's conference in Boston. She told a story about walking into the kitchen and seeing her husband load the dishwasher. You'd think I'd be thrilled, she joked, but instead she started critiquing the way he was doing it. Ever so gently she instructed him to turn the cups over, put the pots in differently, adjust the dishes just so. Her husband looked at her and said that surely a twenty-first-century dishwasher could get an upside down cup clean.

This wasn't about her husband improperly loading the dirty dishes; it was about Cheryl's need for control.

The audience gave a collective *Aha!,* realizing that we've all been guilty at some point of doing the same thing at home and at work. Sometimes we refuse to let others do things their way. We want it done our way, which is a form of control.

Make a list of all the things you must do every week, from making breakfast to doing the laundry to handling chores for an elderly parent to reviewing homework for your kids to getting to the gym to meetings at work. Be specific. (*Hint:* It won't fit on a single sheet of paper.) Then count the number of tasks on your list.

Honestly, you have to laugh. If someone else showed you that list, you would tell him or her it's impossible to get it all done.

Why do we think we have to do it all on our own? Have you ever said or thought one of the following statements?

- "My mom got it all done. Why can't I?"

- "If I don't do it, no one else will."

- "It would take too long to explain. It's just easier if I do it myself."

- "It gets done right only when I do it."

Sound familiar? Let's take them one by one.

- Maybe you're wearing rose-colored glasses when remembering your mom's ability to handle it all. Would she remember it the same way? Probably not.

- Trust me, if you don't do the laundry and your family finds themselves without clothes, they won't go out of the house naked. Someone will figure out how to run a load.

- Even if it were true that something would take longer to explain than to do, explain how to do it anyway. Investing in one explanation may mean that chore will be off your list forever.

- Are you really the only person who can request no starch at the dry cleaners? Sort the recycling? Prepare a meal? I doubt it.

What three chores do you do by yourself because you don't think anyone else could do it as well as you?

1. _____

2. _____

3. _____

What's the worst that would happen if you stopped doing each of those chores?

1. _____

2. _____

3. _____

What daily or weekly task do you honestly feel only you can do?

1. _____

And what would happen if someone else did it?

1. _____

If I said that you absolutely must delegate three tasks at home, what would they be and to whom would you assign them?

1. _____

2. _____

3. _____

Try to delegate at least those three tasks today. See how it feels to have someone else run the dishwasher after dinner. When it's time to empty the load, they'll learn to scrape the plates next time if they're forced to eat off one with last night's tomato sauce still on it. Let someone else fold the laundry—mismatched socks and all. Maybe your sibling can take over one of the duties related to your aging parents. Whatever the assignments, try handing them off to another person.

How else can you enlist that dream team? Maybe you could cover the bake sales or shopping for school supplies in exchange for another parent taking on carpool duties. You can order your groceries online, sparing yourself Saturdays in the supermarket. Use automatic bill paying for those monthly expenses that don't need to be checked. Get your holiday cards preprinted. If you can afford it, look into a virtual concierge (see Chapter 6). I'm sure you can come up with a lot more.

Kisses Make It All Worthwhile

"Work and motherhood? Nothing that a glass of Riesling can't help," jokes Cindy Simmons, a popular radio talk show host on Star94 in Atlanta.

Each time I'm in Atlanta, Cindy and her on-air partner, Ray Mariner, welcome me so graciously to their studio to promote the local Women For Hire events. (My friend Robyn Spizman is a regular at the station, where she hosts a program called the *Giftionary*. And because Cindy and Ray love Robyn, they kindly extend that warmth to me.)

One highlight of every visit is seeing photos of Cindy's daughter and hearing stories about what she is up to. "Honestly, if I had known a year ago that having a little one and a career would have been this rewarding I would have gotten started with mommyhood much earlier," Cindy says.

Cindy knows every career woman faces the whirlwind of meetings, deadlines, and pressure. But at the end of the day, Mom has just one deadline to focus on: "How many kisses can you fit in before you say good night?"

"I will take that kind of pressure any day," she says.

PUT YOURSELF ON YOUR TO-DO LIST

Earlier this year, First Lady Michelle Obama sat down with Oprah Winfrey for an interview in O magazine. Mrs. Obama said, "After I had Malia, I began to prioritize exercise because I realized that my happiness is tied to how I feel about myself. I want my girls to see a mother who takes care of herself, even if that means I have to get up at 4:30 so I can do workouts."

In other words, it's all about tradeoffs and managing your own expectations with those around you. Put yourself on your list.

Everyone you know has some special activity they love to do. Kids may have team sports, music lessons, movies with their friends on the weekend, and more. Your best friend may go running every morning, play golf every weekend, or watch every Bond movie on TV.

When was the last time you really wanted to do something in the past year but didn't get to it? Take yoga? Learn a new language? Play ball with pals? Go out for a monthly dinner with your friends? List three things you'd really love to do in the next three months, along with how much time you'd need to devote in a week to do it.

1. _____

2. _____

3. _____

Can you really not clear your schedule for that brief amount of time to give something back to yourself? Whether it's nature or nurture, most women feel they have to take care of their homes and family at the expense of caring for themselves.

Think about the instructions that flight attendants give before take-off. They tell passengers to put the oxygen mask over their mouth before helping those who need assistance. You can't help your family if you're suffocating from too much work and too much stress. You need me-time, too. It is critical to reboot, reenergize, and refresh your brain or you'll be useless to everyone.

Schedule in this me-time as part of your daily, weekly, or even monthly routine. Everyone around you will be better for it.

TAKE A TIME-OUT

I did a *Good Morning America* segment with Diane Sawyer about the importance of shutting off all electronics at dinnertime—no TV, phones, computers, or BlackBerries. My husband and children, who jokingly refer to themselves as "BlackBerry orphans" because I'm addicted to that small gadget, watched the segment screaming at the screen, "Practice what you preach, Mom!" My husband even sent an e-mail to Diane outing me; she replied that they should install a "truth cam" at home to bust me next time.

The point I learned (really this time) is that when you're having family time—be truly engaged. Distractions from those precious moments don't go unnoticed.

LEARN TO SAY NO

You don't have to be the cookie mom, den dad, class parent, neighborhood committee chair, and more. You don't have to accept every invitation to a holiday party. Sometimes you just have to say no and feel okay about it. Not cramming another appointment or task on your list can feel very empowering.

> **Blah:** "I'm always exhausted because I run myself ragged trying to get it all done."
>
> **Ah!:** "I'm not willing to sacrifice sleep or sanity, so I'm perfectly content doing the best I can."

Now, on to work.

DELEGATE AT WORK

Assigning tasks to others is not just for home, it's for work, too. Take a look at those questions I asked earlier and answer them for the workplace. Any wiggle room in what you take on versus what you really need to be doing? Can those tasks be delegated to a co-worker?

Even if you're not in a position to delegate at work, try to find ways to do something to lessen the load. The most productive people in the office are doing it, maybe even delegating to you. If you are being overloaded, you have to raise your hand.

SINGLETONS HAVE RIGHTS, TOO

Some of my most memorable days have started with my husband and I walking our kids to school. It's several blocks of hand-holding and talking about all sorts of things—from the out-of-state license plates we spot to what we might have for dinner. When we reach the bus stop, we do a short math exercise or trivia question out loud before hugs and kisses good-bye.

It gives me a daily glimpse at how other working moms handle their morning routine. Some appear to be so outwardly harried that you wonder how they ever got out of the house. Others are pictures of calm—despite the previous two hours of insanity that may have preceded their arrival. While I applaud the latter, I'm sure all of us can relate to the former: How many times have we come within a millimeter of losing it ourselves?

Women without kids might find it hard to relate to what I'm describing. I routinely hear from them: They resent all the fuss— the coddling—that society makes over working parents. They complain about accommodations and benefits arranged exclusively for working moms. They're bitter about having to pick up the slack when a mom or dad attends a soccer game and just assumes it's okay to leave a deadline-sensitive project to others to finish.

I understand that. I was single once, and I put in my fair share of 12-hour days when my working parent colleagues routinely punched in and out like clockwork.

No group should be rewarded at the expense of another. Just as working moms should not be penalized for taking care of their kids, their counterparts without kids shouldn't be loaded down with more work and less perks for not having offspring to tend.

When I interviewed her for *Women For Hire* magazine, I asked Beth Brooke, Ernst & Young's global vice chair of strategy, communications, and regulatory affairs, if she thought not having kids had an impact on her extraordinary success.

She told me that it made it a little bit easier for her. "I probably at times in my life was freer to make work choices that maybe had I had children I would not have been able to make. I also know as a single person when all the talk would be about work-life balance, which always oriented around children, I was mentally saying, 'Wait a minute. Single people have incredible challenges. Nobody's doing all the household stuff for me. I've got it all.' "

None of us should feel that benefits and accommodations are entitlements, but rather advantages that we earn through our performance and a business justification. Not every position or employer is able to support all of our personal needs—nor should they have to.

If you're a working parent, be considerate of your childless colleagues. Don't assume that they've got more free time than you do. Don't ask them for favors if you're not willing to reciprocate.

To those without kids my message is the same: offer to pitch in, but only when you feel that your time and help will be appreciated and reciprocated if and when you need it.

> Blah: "People without kids should pick up the slack for working parents because they have fewer responsibilities."

> Ah!: "All employees have to contribute equally. Everyone has interests and responsibilities outside of work."

How to Blend

DEFINE YOUR OWN PROMOTION

In the most traditional sense, a promotion is a step up the ladder with a bigger title, greater responsibility, and more money. But for some people, more responsibility at work doesn't always translate to more satisfaction in life. If you don't want that added responsibility, and if the extra money means you'll be working longer hours, it may not be such a reward after all.

None of this means you should stay put; rather it's a sign that you must define your own version of promotion. Think of your professional and personal advancement in broader terms. A true promotion could be a lateral move that affords a great perk, such as the ability to work from home or tuition reimbursement. It may also mean a lateral move to another role, which would give you a fresh challenge and the opportunity to develop broader skills. A promotion could involve a shift in responsibilities as opposed to the addition of more work.

Keep this in mind as you aim for your next position. Avoid assuming you're taking a step back as if that were always a negative. Instead, think of a career lattice instead of a ladder, on which you can move in multiple directions based on what's best for you at any given time.

Be Open to Change

Marketing executive Lara Hall started her career as a recreation therapist working with seniors. Her job didn't pay well, but she loved it. Then her company was purchased by a larger firm with a greater focus on marketing, meaning she would be expected to split her time between care and promotion.

"I kept the fifty–fifty split for four months or so, but I'd definitely caught the marketing bug. The wheels started turning in my mind: I had a new career possibility ahead of me—one that I had never envisioned before.

"One of the psychologists I worked with asked me to join him as marketing director of a new, cutting-edge care facility. I've been in marketing ever since and love it. You never can tell where life will lead you."

FLEXIBILITY IN THE OFFICE

I am a major proponent of all things flex—a flexible work arrangement between you and your employer that can allow you to have a say in where, when, and how you work. Companies adopt flex-time policies because it helps them retain good employees and spares them from the costs of hiring and retraining new workers. Not only that, but employers recognize the enormous demands outside the office that most of us face. If we're not given the leeway to meet our home obligations, our work suffers because we're not at our best.

As you consider your next employer, research whether flexible programs are offered. This information is typically touted on a company website. You may also get a sense of the culture. If the company doesn't offer a flex-time option for the position you're seeking, it'll be up to you to come up with a plan to propose to your future boss. You have to be creative and considerate when proposing such an arrangement; after all, it's easier for the boss to keep the status quo. Similarly, you have to avoid appearing to want to work less before you even get started, especially during a recession. But if you present a win-win scenario, you might find him or her willing to discuss it.

Unless you're being heavily wooed or you offer a skill that is super hot and hard to find, don't ask for special accommodations until you've been offered the job. You have to feel out the situation to know when the time is right to bring it up. Once they've made you an offer, you know you're wanted and you hold some of the cards to ask for responsible requests, as discussed in Chapter 8.

DECIDE WHAT YOU REALLY WANT

Do you want to telecommute? Work four longer days and get the fifth off? Maybe miss the morning traffic and come in later (and leave later) to better use the day? Maybe work part-time or job share?

Think through all these possibilities, and any others you come up with, and decide on what would really make your life easier. Once you make that decision, it's time to prepare your pitch.

I DESERVE IT

Remember that for many companies, flex-time is an accommodation, not a right. For your boss to allow you this special treatment, you have to convince him or her that you deserve it and that it'll serve the company well, too. It's not just what's best for you; the impact on the organization is paramount.

It's crucial that you are considered a top performer on the job. If the boss doesn't feel he or she can trust you to get the work done without supervision, forget it. However, if you've proven yourself to be a solid, reliable force in your previous positions, you stand a better chance to get this special consideration.

DO YOUR HOMEWORK

Are any of your future co-workers on flex-time? Ask if you can speak to them about their schedules and how they approached the boss to get it. (You may also use your network to find former employees from the company to ask them about similar arrangements.) Find out how flexible work arrangements at other companies in the same industry or the same area are structured and how they are perceived. Proof of success will help immeasurably.

DON'T EXPECT A YES

It's very possible that your new boss will request that you start the job before any kind of special arrangement is approved. He or she may argue that you'll need both hands on deck full-time in the office to ensure your ultimate success. If this is the response, try to nail a time frame for revisiting the request. Perhaps the three-month mark is a good time to sit down again.

If you start a new position without a flexible arrangement in place, it doesn't mean you're out of luck for the long haul. Get in there and wow them, which increases your chances of a warm reception to the idea the next time around.

Prepare for Round Two

TOUT YOUR EARLY SUCCESSES

When you're ready to revist the issue of flex-time, make a list of the contributions you've made since joining the company. This includes your ability to establish relationships and adapt to the protocols.

POWER IN NUMBERS

Are there other workers interested in a flex-time schedule? Create and present your proposal together. Any good boss would sit up and listen if a group of employees request an accommodation that will benefit the company as well as its workers.

PREPARE FOR THE NO

Before you walk in the boss's office, think of all the possible reasons he or she may reject you. Possible problems might be a boss's fear that he or she will lose control of the staff, that you won't be available at short notice to handle an emergency, that clients will miss face time with you or—the most common hesitation—"if I do it for you, I'll have to do it for everyone."

Take these concerns seriously and address them in your proposal. There are answers for all of these concerns, some solved by technology, others by trust, and finally, not every job lends itself to this adjustment and not everyone will want it.

LOOK ON THE BRIGHT SIDE

Employers want their workers to do their jobs well. Seize on that desire by showing your enthusiasm for your job and your certainty that flex-time will improve your job performance. Instead of saying what's wrong with the current arrangement, focus on what will be even better if you make the change, such as more time devoted to work instead of commuting. Stress that this new system is a win-win.

GIVE IT A TRY

Suggest giving it a go for a trial period with defined criteria that must be met to measure the success of your plan. Tell the boss that you understand that the new situation has to be mutually beneficial and that you're open to make changes so that everyone is satisfied. Starting with a temporary arrangement will make is easier for the boss to say yes to a permanent change.

PUT IT ON PAPER

This is a major change for you and your boss, and it deserves a formal presentation outlining the reasons why you're asking for flex-time, how it will benefit everyone involved. Detail your understanding of what is expected of each party during the trial period.

If you make your proposal orally, you risk forgetting key details and backing down too quickly out of nervousness. Also, if your boss has to send the proposal up the chain of command, it's your document that will be telling the story, not a quickly written e-mail that might not present your plan in the best light.

The box below shows a template for a flex-time proposal. Use it to get started and adjust it to fit your purposes.

Flex-Time Proposal Cover Memo

TO: [First name, last time, and title of your boss]
FROM: [Your first name, last name and title, plus those of any of colleagues making the request with you]
DATE: [Today's date]
SUBJECT: Flexible Work Proposal

I would like to request a meeting to discuss my proposal for moving from my current full-time on-site work schedule to a more flexible arrangement.

As you know, I currently work [number] hours at the office each week. I am proposing a shift in my schedule that I'm confident will benefit the company and myself.

The shift would allow me to work from my home office [number] days a week. Communication would be uninterrupted and my productivity would remain strong. I would continue to deliver the quality results you've come to expect from me.

I've given this proposal a great deal of thought as to the benefits for the company and me. I've also researched how similar arrangements work

---

> at our top competitors, which I've used in drafting my proposal, which
> you'll find attached. This outlines how such an arrangement could work,
> addressing potential concerns as well as advantages.
>
> Thank you for considering my proposal. I look forward to speaking with
> you soon to discuss it further. I will be in touch to set a meeting time.

PROPOSED PLAN

Detail how the plan would work: the adjustment in hours or days
and how you plan to split your on-site and at-home tasks. Describe
these arrangements in an upbeat tone that explains how it will benefit the company, with less emphasis on how it will serve *your* needs.

COMMUNICATION

Lay out a detailed plan for communication with the office and your
clients from a technical standpoint. You might request a BlackBerry
or PDA and be willing to share the cost with the company. You can
request access to the office network, propose regular times to check in
with your supervisor, or commit to preparing a weekly status report
to reassure all that your work is being done. Share details about
your home office setup. Do you have a dedicated office space with
a top-of-the-line computer, high-speed Internet access, and a private
phone line? How will key contacts be able to reach you? What if
you're needed in the office on your off day—how will colleagues and
clients find you and what kind of response will you offer?

BENEFITS

This is perhaps the most crucial section, because it outlines how
the arrangement will succeed for the company. Think in terms of

productivity, focus, uninterrupted work time, and anything else that will assure your employer that this arrangement will be an improvement on the current system. If you save two hours each way in commuting time, will you devote some of that to the company? Will working independently enable you to generate even greater results?

TRIAL PERIOD

Suggest that the arrangement be put into effect for a specific trial period, at the end of which you and the boss can assess what works and what doesn't with the plan. While your ultimate goal may be to work from home four days a week full-time, the trial could be set up for two days a week from home for three months. Show a willingness to make adjustments during and after the trial period.

EVALUATION PROCESS

Include a detailed evaluation process, such as weekly or monthly reports from you to your manager that detail your perception of the new relationship. Indicate a willingness to meet at his or her convenience to hear feedback on how the arrangement is working from management's perspective.

WHAT IF THE ANSWER IS NO?

If your plan is rejected, don't throw a tantrum. Ask why, and see if there are tweaks that can be made to the proposal that would make your boss (or his or her boss) more comfortable. Ask if you can supply more information about how well flex-time works at other companies. The goal is to establish a time frame and benchmarks for revisiting the issue in the future. You may set a date or learn the specific business milestones that must be met before this arrangement will be considered.

> Blah: "If the boss doesn't approve my request for a flexible work arrangement, it's proof that this company just gives lip service to balance."

> Ah!: "If the boss doesn't say yes to my request, I'm going to work with her to understand her hesitation, and I'll address her concerns to come to a mutual understanding."

Combining Work and Family on the Job

Another way to blend home and work is *copreneurship*, which is defined as married and in business together. It's definitely not for everybody. Plenty of couples cherish their time apart and couldn't fathom the thought of sharing both personally and professionally. The ability to find a partner with whom to create a happy home *and* a thriving business is somewhat magical. Listen to your head and your heart to know if such an arrangement might work for you.

It works for me. Last year my husband, Peter, joined me at Women For Hire. Even though he's been my biggest cheerleader from a distance and he's knowledgeable about all things related to my work, the company has always been my baby, not his.

We had toyed with the idea for years that he should give up the only career he had ever known—newspaper journalism—so we could work together. The curiosity, challenge, and fun in his line of work had dissipated, and it was high time for Act Two. Yet, it's always scary to pull the trigger and up and quit. Both of us were gun-shy.

But at the end of 2007, *USA Today,* his employer of nearly 30 years, made a one-time offer that he simply couldn't refuse: A somewhat generous voluntary buyout. They were paying him to leave. Woo hoo!

While our kids knew what was going on, we were scared to tell extended family. The reactions would be predictable: Are you sure this is a good idea? Won't you hate being together 24/7? How will Peter feel going from being a national columnist at the biggest paper in the country to an unknown at a small shop nobody's heard of?

We played the cynics' questions over and over and continued to come to the same conclusion: We were confident this was the right move for us. We weren't naive enough to assume this arrangement would be without some challenges, and we've taken measures to address them.

Even though we work in an open office with nine other desks, a half wall separates Peter and me. This provides just enough privacy and space. While we try not to fight in front of colleagues, we hardly yes each other either; we're perfectly willing to reject one another's harebrained ideas.

Each of us has distinct roles and responsibilities that build on our individual strengths and expertise. And perhaps most important, we respect each other. This business partnership works because we don't just love like husband and wife; we really like each other as best friends, too.

Don't Be Afraid to Ask for Help

Shannon Wilburn, founder of Just Between Friends Franchise Systems, says that trying to do everything as a small business owner is counter-productive and a good way to burn yourself out.

"You don't have to be an expert in everything and you don't have to do it all yourself," says Shannon, whose company enables moms to buy and sell used kids clothing and accessories. "I tried to be all things to all people, and I failed."

Shannon says she insisted on doing her own finances and accounting.

But as Just Between Friends grew, the finances became too over-whelming for her to handle alone. "We hired a bookkeeper and an accountant. It allowed me to focus on building my business. It was so freeing.

"I thought I had to do it all, but I didn't," Shannon says. "Rely on people who are good at what they do, and focus on what you are good at. Once I realized I didn't have to do it all, my business really took off—because I was willing to let go and let others help."

IS IT FOR YOU?

Do a lot of soul searching and talk candidly about this kind of arrangement before you pull the trigger. Figure out who'll handle what and define distinct responsibilities so you're not stepping on toes. Understand that there will be a learning curve for both of you. Agree on an exit strategy in advance in case the good intentions don't work out.

Blending your home and work lives takes a big commitment from both of you. Asking for help at home and for accommodations at work may not be easy. But the payoff can be enormous.

Now sit down with a cup of coffee, and do the exercises in this chapter—the first steps in getting the best life for you and your family. Turn up the volume on Gloria Gaynor's "I Am What I Am" and blast James Brown's "I Feel Good" on the stereo or your iPod and resolve to throw your battered superhero cape in the trash.

CHAPTER 11

Pay It Forward

Give an inch or go a mile

You make a living by what you get. You make a life by what you give.
—WINSTON CHURCHILL

During your job search, you may reach out to hundreds of people. Some will be forthcoming with contacts and leads, others will need to be charmed before they give you the help you need. However, there are those who eagerly share their time and experience; remember this as a gift that you must pass along.

I read a passage in Maya Angelou's recent book *Letter to My Daughter*. In it she writes, "That day I learned that I could be a giver by simply bringing a smile to another person. The ensuing years have taught me that a kind word, a vote of support is a charitable gift."

We all have the ability to do just that. Paying it forward is by no means limited to giving someone a job or donating big bucks to a particular cause.

If you have found a job, it might be hard to help with someone else's job search because remembering the uncertainty and the fear can be unsettling. Get over that and try to support others. Smart people pay it forward. You not only create good career karma for yourself but the person you extended a hand to may be your boss someday.

Yes, it's easier to say, "I don't have time" than to make a half-hour coffee date and open your contact file. It's easier to ignore e-mails asking for career advice. Don't do it. Share your contacts and experience. You don't have to be some high-powered executive with a big title and six-figure salary to be of value to a job seeker. You're probably mentoring someone already without realizing it—your children, family, friends, or former co-workers. Become a mentor to a colleague or someone trying to change careers or reenter the workforce. The relationship need not be based on age: Although older professionals can mentor younger colleagues, reverse mentoring is just as powerful. Your encouragement and support will make an enormous difference to someone trying to get his or her career on track.

How to Give

FORMAL GIVING: ONE ON ONE

Once you've identified someone you think could benefit from a little help, take the time to make a personal connection. Let it be known that you're available to talk. Show that you are approachable, sincere, and eager to help.

Once that is established, listen. Being a giver doesn't mean that you should lecture the person about what she's doing wrong; just be a sounding board. Just listening may reveal your mentee's roadblock, what's stopping her from getting the job she wants. Then you can offer examples of similar dilemmas you've faced and share how you've tackled the problem. Candor, communication, and trust are the most important elements in being an effective mentor.

So go ahead, e-mail a colleague to offer your ear or get up from your computer and chat in person. You're likely to find an appreciative response at the other end. And you'll be well on your way to enjoying the rich and rewarding benefit of knowing that you did a very good deed for someone in need.

MAKE YOURSELF AVAILABLE TO NEW GRADS

Your alma mater is always looking for professionals who are willing to offer informational interviews. When you call the alumni relations office to ask about contacts for your own job search, indicate that you, too, are willing to talk to current students or alumni about their job searches. I'm involved with Emerson College— serving on the alumni board of directors and mentoring students informally. I often receive e-mails from new grads looking for help landing a job. My responses range from critiquing their résumé and cover letter to offering specific leads and direction to assist with their goals.

GIVE TO CYBER STRANGERS

Sometimes the Women For Hire message boards get a bit heated with lively give-and-take. Other times—these are my favorite moments—there's a genuine back-and-forth with women helping one another, sharing resources, and offering support. I see the same thing among men and women on the *Good Morning America* message boards as well.

On LinkedIn, where there are thousands of groups you can join and participate in, I manage a Women For Hire group with more than 10,000 members who exchange advice every day. There's a real camaraderie among total strangers—all of whom are hoping to learn and benefit from one another. It's all free, so if you've ever wanted to mentor someone but don't know where to start or how to get involved, this is a simple step, no long-term commitment, no strings attached. Sign on to the message boards in your industry or the ones aligned with your personal and professional interests and reply to postings with your best ideas and advice.

CELEBRATE THE VICTORIES

No matter where you live or the kind of work you do, always be supportive of other people's success. Celebrate when someone lands a job or gets a promotion. Encourage that person to feel great about his or her accomplishment. This is especially important for women, many of whom tend to downplay achievements. When she attempts to do just that by saying, "Oh it was nothing" or, "My role wasn't really a big deal," stop her in her tracks. Tell her, "I won't allow you to run from your successes. I insist that you claim them—and we'll celebrate together!" It may sound oh-so-hokey, but it's essential for workplace growth.

When you help another woman feel great about herself or when you help her to accomplish her goals, that one gesture for that one person goes much further. When a woman is in a good place, she typically repays it in dividends: to her family, to her friends, to her colleagues, to her community. Both men and women can contribute to that chain of goodwill.

Friends and family often tell me that I should sleep well at night for the work I do helping people find jobs and advising others on their careers. It's wonderful to hear. But more often than not I worry about those e-mails I didn't get to answer or the people who really require a lot of hand-holding to get back on their feet. There are only so many hours in the day, and I wish I could do more, but I can't allow that to take away from the victories big and small as they come.

I get great satisfaction reporting on workplace issues on *Good Morning America,* hosting dozens of Women For Hire career fairs across the country each year, giving speeches about workplace success, posting on blogs, making videos, and contributing other valuable information on our website, WomenForHire.com.

I hope this book has helped you gain the skills, confidence, and energy to keep searching for the job that suits your needs. The country is facing very hard times, but I want you to know the right job is out there, and you will find it. And once you've secured that position, it will do you and the country a lot of good if you help a neighbor in need to find a job, too.

Know that I wish you all good things as you venture down that path and that I'm rooting for your greatest success. Download U2's "One" and "This One's for the Girls" by Martina McBride for some added inspiration.

A Final Thought

On our website WomenForHire.com, we feature a series of audio interviews with dynamic women. The purpose is to offer short bursts of success for visitors to hear how someone else did it and to showcase tips and tricks for everyone to benefit from.

One of my all-time favorites from the series comes from Gayle King, O magazine's editor-at-large and Oprah Winfrey's best friend. Gayle told us that while she has a fabulous life, with no complaints, she never believes that this is as good as it gets. She says that no matter how much money you have, how much success you've achieved, how great you think things are, it's a bad day if you start thinking this is as good as it gets. It means you give up, you stop trying, and you stop learning.

Now you may be thinking, "Thank goodness this is not as good as it gets, otherwise I'm in big trouble." We all have those days. I know I do.

Gayle's message is an important one for all of us, no matter what our work situation may be: Try to make today better than yesterday and use what you learn today in hopes of making tomorrow even better.

Even though I don't know you, I bet you subscribe in some way to that philosophy, which is why you chose to read this book. I applaud you for embracing the idea and doing everything you can to make your best days the ones that lay ahead.

That's the mission of Women For Hire and the goal of this book. Get out there, meet new people, reconnect with old friends, and stay open to new possibilities. The best opportunities don't simply appear out of thin air by chance. They happen because you deliberately chose to put yourself in a position to be receptive to them. You have the ability to make wonderful things happen for yourself. You hold the power to realize your workplace goals.

ACKNOWLEDGMENTS

The love and laughter of my husband, Peter, and our children, Emma, Jake, and Nick, keep me sane and smiling amid the organized chaos surrounding our life. My brother, David, works tirelessly day and night to support my work and my sister-in-law, Julie, is my greatest cheerleader. I'm grateful to the women who have significant roles in making what we do at Women For Hire possible—Dora Dvir, Donna Weitz, Stephanie Biasi, Amanda Donikowski, Michelle Atkins, Lindsay More Nisbett, and Margaret Johnson. Since day one my mom, Sherry Beilinson, has been the not-so-secret weapon who makes sure that every event we host is planned and executed with extraordinary care so that everyone who comes through our doors is in good hands.

I'm an exceptionally lucky girl to have Diane Sawyer champion my work. Robin Roberts always reminds me how important all of this is to so many people. Everyone at *Good Morning America,* especially Anna Robertson, has given me the greatest gift of an enormous platform to educate and assist our audience on job searching and workplace issues. The teams at ABCNews.com and ABC News Now are tops.

Credit for encouraging me to write this book goes to Meredith Bernstein, my literary agent, and Robyn Spizman, my dear friend with whom I shared the excitement of a *New York Times* bestseller when we cowrote *Will Work from Home: Earn the Cash—Without the Commute.*

Sincere appreciation to my editor, Adrienne Avila, at Berkley Publishing of the Penguin Group for her guidance and clear vision—and to the talented team at Berkley, including publisher Leslie Gelbman, managing editor Pam Barricklow, copyeditor Candace B. Levy, book designer Tiffany Estreicher, cover designer Diana Kolsky, and the public relations team of Craig Burke, Julia Fleischaker, Rick Pascocello, and Erica Colon.

I couldn't have managed this project without the incredible talent and humor of Laura Zaccaro, my right hand in organizing, researching, and writing.

And finally, to all the women I've met in the last 10 years since founding Women For Hire, you've shown me that, whether you're a highly educated big-city girl or a small-town gal whose circumstances prevented you from finishing high school, a new mom or an empty nester returning to the workplace, a mechanical engineer or a manicurist, we all share the same goal: to provide for ourselves and our loved ones and to secure our future. I hope some of my work enables many of you to do just that.

RESOURCES

In addition to WomenForHire.com of course, here's a selection of some of my other favorite resources to assist with your job search.

Resources to Make You Feel Better About You

EWOMEN NETWORK'S GLOW PROJECT:

TheGlowProject.org

FIND A SPIRIT BOOST AMONG OPINIONATED WOMEN:

Career.Alltop.com

WowoWow.com

Shine.Yahoo.com

NATIONAL FOUNDATION FOR CREDIT COUNSELING:

DebtAdvice.org

Resources to Enable You to Build Your Profile and Declare Your Expertise

BLOG SITES:

Blogger.com

BlogHer.com

Tumblr.com

WordPress.com

BUILD YOUR DIGITAL IDENTITY:

Facebook.com

LinkedIn.com

MySpace.com

Ning.com

Twitter.com

BUSINESS CARDS:

GotPrint.com

Kinkos.com

Staples.com

VistaPrint.com

CREATE A VISUAL/DIGITAL RESUME:

VisualCV.com

DOMAIN REGISTRATION AND WEBSITE TOOLS:

Register.com

GoDaddy.com

Resources to Connect You with New Contacts

GET THE BEST TIPS ON WORKING ANY ROOM:

SusanRoane.com

FIND JUST ABOUT ANYONE YOU WANT TO MEET:

Facebook.com

LinkedIn.com

Twitter.com

FIND PEOPLE ON TWITTER.COM IN YOUR FIELD OF INTEREST:

Search.Twitter.com

Twellow.com

ORGANIZE YOUR CONTACTS AND KEEP TRACK OF JOB SEARCH COMMUNICATION:

Google.com/docs

JibberJobber.com

KEEP UP WITH WHAT'S HAPPENING IN THE WORLD AND BUSINESS:

ABCNews.com

Bloomberg.com

CEOExpress.com

CNBC.com

News.Google.com

Newser.com

TheDailyBeast.com

WSJ.com

Resources to Assist with Your Job Search

CAREER ASSESSMENT TOOLS (FREE AND FEE-BASED):

Assessment.com

CareerPlanner.com

ImproveNow.com

Keirsey.com

LiveCareer.com

JoBehaviors.com

WhatHalf.com

KnowYourType.com

HumanMetrics.com

GIANT JOB BOARDS:

CareerBuilder.com

HotJobs.com

Monster.com

JOB BOARD AGGREGATORS (BRING TOGETHER JOB BOARD LISTINGS FOR ONE-STOP SEARCHING):

Indeed.com

SimplyHired.com

LOCAL NEWSPAPER ONLINE JOB BOARDS: (LOOK UP YOUR LOCAL PAPER ONLINE.)

Boston Globe: bostonworks.com

Houston Chronicle: chron.com/class/jobs

Los Angeles Times: latimes.com/classified/jobs

New York Times: jobmarket.nytimes.com

Wall Street Journal: careers.wsj.com

SPECIALTY INDUSTRY NICHE SITES:

Creative positions: CreativeHeads.net; CreativePro.com

Executive positions: TheLadders.com; 6figurejobs.com

Finance positions: JobsintheMoney.com; FinancialJobs.com

Government positions: USAJobs.gov

Human Resource positions: Jobs.SHRM.org; HRJobs.com; Jobs
.ERE.net

Marketing positions: MarketingPower.com; MarketingJobs.com

Media positions: MediaBistro.com; Mandy.com

Nonprofit positions: Idealist.org; NonProfitJobs.org

Off the beaten path positions: JobMonkey.com; BackDoorJobs.com

Part-time or hourly positions: SnagaJob.com, WorkinRetail.com

Post-college positions: Experience.com; JobTrak.com, CollegeRecruiter
.com

Technology jobs: Dice.com; ComputerJobs.com

**LINKS TO JUST ABOUT EVERY JOB BOARD AND A WIDE RANGE
OF CAREER RESOURCES:**

Job-hunt.org

JobHuntersBible.com

Weddles.com

Jobstar.org

RileyGuide.com

QuintCareers.com

DIVERSITY JOB BOARDS:

DiversityInc.com

HireDiversity.com

Latpro.com

WomenForHire.com

NATIONAL STAFFING FIRMS (FIND LOCAL ONES IN YOUR AREA VIA GOOGLE):

Adecco.com

Administaff.com

KellyServices.com

RobertHalf.com

Spherion.com

StaffingToday.net

FLEXIBLE PLACEMENT FIRMS:

Aquent.com

FlexJobs.com

MomCorps.com

TentilTwo.com

COMPANY RESEARCH TOOLS:

CEOExpress.com

Hoovers.com

Vault.com

WetFeet.com

Resources to Overcome Career-Related Obstacles

AGE-RELATED JOB BOARDS AND SEARCH RESOURCES:

AARP.org

ExperienceWorks.org

RetirementJobs.com

Workforce50.com

YourEncore.com

RETURNSHIP PROGRAM AT SARA LEE:

SaraLee.com/WorkingAtSaraLee/ReturnshipProgram.aspx

HIGHER EDUCATION AND TRAINING PROGRAMS:

CareerOneStep.gov

CareerStep.com

CareerVoyages.gov

ELearners.com

ForteFoundation.org

MBATour.com

OCWConsortium.com

RETURNING MOMS:

JobsandMoms.com

ExecutiveMoms.com

iRelaunch.com

MomCorps.com

On-Ramps.com

FREE CREDIT REPORTS:

AnnualCreditReport.com

Resources to Find Other Job Seekers Looking to Join Forces

ABC News Job Club with Tory Johnson

ABCNews.com/JobClub

FEE-BASED NETWORKING GROUPS:

Execunet.com

FiveOClockClub.com

Resources for Making Money from Home

FREELANCE MARKETPLACE:

Craigslist.com

Crossloop.com

Elance.com

Guru.com

Odesk.com

VIRTUAL CUSTOMER SERVICE AGENTS:

AlpineAccess.com

Arise.com

LiveOps.com

Teleperformance.com

VIPDesk.com

WestatHome.com

WorkingSolutions.com

VIRTUAL ASSISTANTS AND TRAVEL AGENTS:

WTH.com

TeamDoubleClick.com

VANetworking.com

IVAA.org

ELDERCARE, BABYSITTING AND PET-SITTING SERVICES:

Care.com

Care4Hire. com

FetchPetCare.com

HomeInstead.com

RightAtHome.net

SeniorHelpers.com

SitterCity.com

SunriseSeniorLiving.com

POCKET CHANGE FOR ONLINE GUIDES:

Chacha.com

JustAnswer.com

LivePerson.com

DIRECT SELLING ASSOCIATION:

DirectSelling411.com

(A more comprehensive list of home-based opportunities can be found in *Will Work From Home: Earn the Cash—Without the Commute* and on WomenForHire.com.)

Resources to Help You Start a Business

START-UP ADVICE:

Collective-E.com

MakeMineAMillion.org

NAWBO.org

OpenForum.com

SBA.gov

SBTV.com

SCORE.org

StartupJournal.com

StartupNation.com

WorkingSolo.com

START-UP PUBLICITY:

HelpAReporter.com

START-UP MONEY:

Mint.com

Prosper.com

VirginMoneyUS.com

START-UP BUSINESS NEEDS:

LogoEase.com

LogoMaker.com

Register.com or GoDaddy.com

VerticalResponse.com

Resources to Ask for Money and Benefits

Carnegie Mellon professor Linda Babcock's website: WomenDontAsk .com

Carol Frohlinger's site, which includes valuable online courses: NegotiatingWomen.com

SALARY DATA AND PAY CALCULATORS:

GlassDoor.com

PayScale.com

Salary.com

Vault.com

Resources to Blend Career and Family to Get the Best of Both

CaliandJody.com (flex concepts from the authors of *Why Work Sucks and How to Fix It*)

CherylRichardson.com

MarthaBeck.com

StressInstitute.com

Resources to Give Back

Women For Hire on LinkedIn.com (Go to LinkedIn.com and search for "Women For Hire")

ONLINE AND OFFLINE MENTORING:

GenConnect.com

GottaMentor.com

Mentoring.org

TaprootFoundation.org

VolunteerMatch.org

A Playlist to Get You in the Mood for Job Search Success

"Beautiful" by Christina Aguilera

"Big Yellow Taxi" by Joni Mitchell

"Breakaway" by Kelly Clarkson

"Dreamer" by John Lennon

"Good Riddance" by Green Day

"Happy" by Natasha Bedingfield

"Help" by The Beatles

"Home" by Daughtry

"I Am What I Am" by Gloria Gaynor

"I Feel Good" by James Brown

"I Want to Talk About Me" by Toby Keith

"I Will Survive" by Gloria Gaynor

"I'll Be There" by the Jackson 5 or Mariah Carey

"It's My Life" by Bon Jovi

"Lean on Me" by Bill Withers

"Listen" by Beyonce

"Man! I Feel Like a Woman" by Shania Twain

"Money" by Pink Floyd

"One" by U2

"Pocketful of Sunshine" by Natasha Bedingfield

"Put Your Records On" by Corinne Bailey Rae

"She Works Hard for the Money" by Donna Summer

"Shiny Happy People" by REM

"Something to Talk About" by Bonnie Raitt

"Start Me Up" by Rolling Stones

"Superwoman" by Alicia Keys

"Survivor" by Destiny's Child

"The Rising" by Bruce Springsteen

"This Is My Now" by Jordin Sparks

"This One's for the Girls" by Martina McBride

"Unwritten" by Natasha Bedingfield

"We Will Rock You" by Queen

PROFESSIONAL SUMMARY AND OBJECTIVE

Your professional summary is your persuasive sales pitch that introduces you to potential employers and allows them to consider you in the context of their hiring needs. Compose three to five sentences touting your key capabilities and unique experience, with an emphasis on results.

EXPERIENCE

Most Recent Job Title   City, State
Employer   (Month Year to Month Year)

Brief overview of your successes relating to the position's main responsibilities, including an explanation of the organization if it's not well known.
• Outline your most impressive accomplishments using bullet points. Focus on the results of your actions, not just your responsibilities. Include industry buzzwords and tangible numbers to support your experience. The eye is drawn to figures, especially on a sales résumé.
• Start every bullet with an impressive action word, and vary words throughout your résumé. Avoid fancy fonts.

Previous Job Title   City, State
Employer   (Month Year to Month Year)

Keep position summaries short and relevant.
• Outline your most important, impressive accomplishments, not a complete menu of every task you've ever performed.
• As a general rule, the amount of information—both summaries and bullets—beneath each position should decrease as you move toward older assignments.
Earlier Job Title   City, State
Employer   (Month Year to Month Year)
• Earlier jobs require minimal information, though they are important to demonstrate career advancement.

EDUCATION

MBA, University (Most recent degree goes on top)
BA, College, 2002 (Date is optional, but usually included especially if it's recent)
• GPA only if it is above 3.5, Honors Received (e.g. magna cum laude or Dean's List)

SKILLS/QUALIFICATIONS

• This section is used to enhance your summary and experience while highlighting specific qualifications that are either required for a particular job or are unique about you.

MEMBERSHIPS/AFFILIATIONS

• This is valuable for everyone, including recent grads and career changers to demonstrate that you're making an effort to establish yourself in a new field.

INDEX

Page numbers in **bold** indicate tables; those in *italic* indicate figures.

ABOUT THE AUTHOR

Career-savvy expert Tory Johnson is the founder and CEO of Women For Hire, the only producer of high-caliber recruiting events connecting professional women with leading employers from IBM to the FBI.

Johnson is also the workplace contributor on ABC's *Good Morning America*, where she has reached millions of viewers since 2005 on a wide range of job-related issues and challenges. She is the anchor of *Job Club* on ABC News Now, a 24-hour digital news channel, and her columns on ABCNews.com are consistently as popular as her on-air segments.

She is a frequent speaker to audiences nationwide, ranging from college campuses and Fortune 500 companies to prestigious conferences, where she shares strategies and solutions for finding success and satisfaction at work.

Glamour magazine dubbed Johnson the "raise fairy godmother" because of her expertise in advising a panel of women on how to successfully ask for—and secure—salary increases.

Johnson's fourth career book, *Will Work from Home: Earn the Cash—Without the Commute* was published in 2008 and became an instant *New York Times* and *Wall Street Journal* bestseller.

As an award-winning business leader, Johnson has been recognized with various honors, ranging from the prestigious Annual Leadership Award from The Women's Center to distinguished alumni achievement awards from Emerson College, where she serves on the Alumni Association Board of Directors.

She is a mentor to dozens of women throughout the country, providing one-on-one guidance for both career advancement and entrepreneurship. In addition to her high-profile work with people displaced by Hurricane Katrina in the Gulf states, she is an active volunteer for many community-based organizations focusing on women's issues and education.

Johnson founded Women For Hire after serving in corporate communications positions at ABC News, NBC News, and Nickelodeon. She lives in New York City with her husband and children.

Connect with her at WomenForHire.com, follow her at Twitter .com/ToryJohnson, and get more of her advice at ABCNews.com /ToryJohnson.

As an exclusive bonus for purchasing this book, Tory Johnson has created a ninety-minute online video seminar featuring all-new advice and resources for job searching and career advancement in a challenging economic climate. Once you buy this book, send your proof of purchase to book@womenforhire.com to receive complimentary access to the exceptional program. Offer is available until December 31, 2009. Visit womenforhire.com for details.

Want Tory Johnson to speak
to your very own job club?

Go to WomenForHire.com and sign up for Tory's newsletter. You can search and post on her job board, snag more career advancement tips, and learn about her upcoming events. And you can even submit a request for Tory to connect with your job club!

Your group may become eligible for Tory to connect by phone or video chat during one of your meetings to address your career challenges.